JOURNEY
with J.W.

John Wesley's Ride
Through Methodist History

For Elementary Children • Reproducibles

Adapted from *J. W. & Co.* Copyright 1997 by Cokesbury.

No part of this work may be reproduced or transmitted in any form or by any means, electronic or mechanical, including photocopying and recording, or by any information storage or retrieval system, except as may be expressly permitted by the 1976 Copyright Act or by permission in writing from the publisher. Requests for permission should be submitted in writing to: Rights and Permissions, The United Methodist Publishing House, 2222 Rosa L. Parks Blvd., PO Box 280988, Nashville, TN 37228-0988; faxed to 615-749-6128; or submitted via e-mail to *permissions@abingdonpress.com*.

Scripture quotations in this publication, unless otherwise indicated, are from the Common English Bible. Copyright © 2011 by the Common English Bible. All rights reserved. Used by permission.

Scripture quotations marked (GNT) are from the Good News Translation in Today's English Version-Second Edition © 1992 by American Bible Society. Used by Permission.

Special thanks to consultants Nancy Spence and Pamela Buchholz.

ISBN: 9781501805066

PACP 10040150-01

Editor/Writer: Daphna Flegal

Research Editor: Vicki Hines

Production Editor: Laura Allison

Designer: Matthew Allison

Bible Stories/Dramas by LeeDell Stickler

Illustrations by Robert S. Jones

15 16 17 18 19 20 21 22 23 24—10 9 8 7 6 5 4 3 2 1

Printed in the U. S. A.

Table of Contents

Introduction

Journey With J.W. is a six-week event that lets your elementary children experience life in the times of John Wesley and the circuit riders. The children are grouped in Holy Clubs. Each Holy Club has a leader. The leader greets the children at the beginning of each session and guides the children to the activities. Plan for no more than eight to twelve children in each club. You may group the children according to ages or mix the ages for a more family feeling. Mixing the ages also allows older children to help younger children.

The village is made of shoppes, the jail, the storytelling area, and the singing school all based on life in the 1700s. The children will visit the shoppes and the jail with their Holy Clubs. If you have a larger group of children and several Holy Clubs, rotate the groups between the shoppes. If you have a smaller group of children, you may want to move them as a whole group. Shopkeepers demonstrate and lead these activities. While the children are enjoying the activities, the shopkeepers share with the children information about the times and the people. The Holy Club leader is there as an additional pair of hands.

During each session all the children will go to the storytelling area. In this area the children will meet a character out of history like Susanna Wesley, hear that character tell a Bible story, and watch or participate in a drama. Plan to have a volunteer coordinate the drama for each week.

The Space

Journey With J.W. may be set up indoors or outdoors. Use a large area like a fellowship hall or gym for the village. All the shoppes are not used in the same session. Different shoppes may be set up in the same space. If you do not have a large enough room for all the shoppes you will use in one session, use individual classrooms and set up one or two shoppes in each room.

All the children will come together to hear the Bible stories and watch the dramas. You will need a stage area, one end of your fellowship hall or gym, or a separate room used only for this activity.

Volunteers

Journey With J.W. uses the gifts and talents of adults in your congregation without overwhelming them. You will need:

- *Holy Club Leaders (one for each Holy Club).*
- *Shopkeepers (at least one for each shoppe).*
- *Characters (see pp. 23, 38, 52, 63, 76):*

  J.W. (John Wesley)   Susanna Wesley

  Charles Wesley   Thomas Coke

  Richard Allen

  Drama Coach (for each session)

  Jailkeeper (pp. 47-48)

J.W.

Recruit someone to play the part of J.W. (John Wesley) throughout the event. Have the person dress up in a costume to indicate men's clothing of the 1700s. The costume may include breeches, knee socks, a full-sleeved shirt, a vest, and a frocked coat. Patterns are available from fabric stores. Or have J.W. dress in a black clergy's robe. Cut a white collar out of felt to wear with the robe. John Wesley had long hair (he did not want to spend his money on hair cuts). You may want J.W. to wear a wig.

J.W. should wander through the village each session. J.W. may stand on a wooden box or in front of one of the village shoppes and begin preaching. Use "John Wesley's Sayings" (p. 80) for suggestions of what he can say. J.W. should speak in a compelling, loud voice for a few minutes each time. Have J.W. hold a Bible as he speaks. He may slip the sayings inside the open Bible.

Snacks

The snacks are handled through the village inn and eaten in Holy Clubs.

Camp Meeting

Have a camp meeting as your closing celebration. Invite friends and families to attend with the children (see Session 6).

Missions

Plan a mission project for the children to participate in during the event. Send home information about the project. Set baskets in the Holy Clubs for the children to place whatever they are bringing for the project. Plan to present the baskets during the closing camp meeting.

> ### Suggested Projects:
> - *Bring canned goods for a food pantry.*
> - *Participate in a prison ministry.*
> - *Participate in the United Methodist Children's Fund for Christian Mission.*

The United Methodist Children's Fund for Christian Mission GBOD P.O. Box 340003 Nashville, TN 37203-0003

Each year the United Methodist Children's Fund chooses six projects to support. Projects are chosen from recommendations by the World, National, and Women's Divisions of the General Board of Global Ministries; the United Methodist Committee on Relief; and individual applications. Selections are made by the General Board of Discipleship and General Board of Global Ministries.

A promotional packet explaining the current projects is available from the address in the column on the left. One copy of the packet is free to a church. Send funds to the same address.

Publicity

Photocopy the following page to use for publicity.

JOURNEY with J.W.

Ride into United Methodist History with John Wesley.

Date: _____   **Time:** _____

Session 1: Susanna Wesley

In this session your children will be introduced to Susanna, John, and Charles Wesley. Susanna was the youngest child of twenty-five children. She married a man named Samuel Wesley, a pastor in the Church of England. Susanna and Samuel had nineteen children, but only ten of the nineteen children lived.

Suggestions for Session 1

1. *Begin the Session in the Holy Clubs, and play the quilt game to help the children meet each other and learn each other's names.*
2. *Move to The Village Shoppes.*
3. *Choose all or some of the following shoppes:*
   The Village Inn: Make Butter
   The Village School: Make Hornbooks
   The Toy Shoppe: Make Thaumatropes
4. *Gather the children into a large group for the activities in The Wesley Home.*
5. *Send the children back to their Holy Clubs to enjoy their snack and close the session.*

Volunteers Needed

- *Holy Club Leaders*
- *Shoppe Leaders: The Village Inn, The Village School, The Toy Shoppe*
- *Charles Wesley*
- *Susanna Wesley*
- *Actors for "Fire!"*

Holy Clubs

The children will be grouped in Holy Clubs. Plan for eight to twelve children in each group.

Each Holy Club has a leader. The leader is responsible for greeting the children at each session, giving the children their nametags, and leading the opening worship. The Holy Club leader should plan to stay with the children and participate with the children in each activity. The children will return to their Holy Clubs to eat their snacks.

✦ Set Up Holy Clubs

Supplies: *p. 15, quilts, can with sand or gravel, dowel or stick*

- *Place quilts on the floor to designate each Holy Club.*
- *Photocopy the "Holy Club" sign (p. 15) for each club.*
- *Set a can beside each quilt. Fill the can with sand or gravel. Add a dowel or stick. Place a Holy Club sign on the dowel or stick. Write a number on each sign. This becomes the Holy Club's number.*
- *Make nametags for the children.*

✦ Quilt Game

Supplies: *p. 16, crayons*

- *Photocopy "Quilt Game" (p. 16) for each Holy Club.*
- *Write the children's names in the spaces provided.*
- *Let each child choose a crayon to be his or her color.*

SAY: In the 1700s people made quilts by sewing together pieces of leftover fabric. Each quilt was unique. God made each of us unique. Let's get to know each other by coloring a quilt that shows some things about us.

- *Read the topics at the top of the game sheet. When the children find topics that are true for them, have them color in those squares on their name lines with their crayons.*
- *Display the quilt from each Holy Club around the room.*

✦ Tell About The Holy Club

SAY: John Wesley was a man who lived in England in the 1700s. John Wesley felt he was called by God to tell others about Jesus and help people in need. He started a religious movement called Methodism. The United Methodist Church is founded on John Wesley's ideas. You may run into a man we call J.W. while you are here. J.W. is John Wesley.

John and his brother, Charles, attended school at Oxford University in England. While Charles was at Oxford, he began the Holy Club. Each member of the Holy Club did these things: got up early; read the Bible; prayed; didn't waste time. Some people nicknamed the club members "methodists" because the members had a method to everything they did. The name *methodist* became the name for people who followed the new religious movement started by John Wesley.

The members of the Holy Club spent time helping others. They visited prisons to read Scripture and pray with the prisoners. The members of the Holy Club also used their own money to buy food, clothing, and medicines for people who were in need.

Let's pretend that we are part of Charles and John Wesley's Holy Club. We'll work and play together to learn about the United Methodist Church.

Involve the children in the quilt game as soon as they arrive.

✦ Missions

- *Tell the children about any mission project your group is doing as part of Journey With J.W.*

✦ Learn the Bible Verse

Supplies: *Bible, beanbag or ball*

> **Therefore, go and make disciples of all nations.**
> *Matthew 28:19*

- *Choose a child to read the Bible verse.*
- *Have all the children repeat the verse.*
- *Have the children sit in a circle. Tell them to pass a beanbag or ball to the children sitting next to them in the circle. The first person to pass the beanbag or ball says the first word of the Bible verse. Have the children keep passing the beanbag or ball around the circle. Each child says the next word of the Bible verse as she or he passes the beanbag or ball.*
- *As the children become familiar with the Bible verse, let them toss the beanbag or ball across the circle at random, saying the words in order.*

The Village Shoppes

The village is made of shoppes, the jail, and the village square, all based on life in the 1700s. The shoppes will include the Village Inn (where snack is made) and one or two other shoppes, depending on the length of time needed for the activity.

The children will visit the shoppes with their Holy Clubs. If you have a large number of Holy Clubs, let the clubs rotate.

Shopkeepers demonstrate and lead these activities. While the children are enjoying the activities, the shopkeeper tells the children information about the times and the people. The Holy Club leader is there as an additional pair of hands.

The Village Inn

Supplies: *baskets, wooden bowls, iron skillets, teapots, and churns*

- *Display baskets, wooden bowls, iron skillets, teapots, and churns.*

SAY: When travelers needed a place to sleep and eat, they often stopped at inns. The main room of the inn was usually filled with tables and benches. People stopped in the main room for food and drink.

Where you slept depended on how much money you had to spend. If you had more money, you could buy a bed with sheets. If not, you might find yourself sleeping on a straw mattress on the floor without any sheets at all. There were no bathrooms. Often travelers shared the same water bucket and the same towel. Travelers also found themselves sharing bedbugs and lice.

✦ *Make Butter*

Supplies: *baby food jars, heavy cream*

- *Collect baby food jars and sterilize in dishwasher.*
- *Let heavy cream (not light whipping cream) warm to room temperature.*

SAY: Butter was made in a churn. A churn looked like a tall wooden bucket. It had a cover with a hole in the middle. A wooden pole fit through the hole so that the top of the pole came up out of the churn. The pole was called the dasher.

Milk was set out to let the cream rise to the top. The cream that rose to the top was skimmed off and saved for whipping cream. The milk was then allowed to sour. The sour milk was poured into the churn. Someone sat and moved the dasher up and down for about an hour. This separated the butter into small lumps.

The lumps rose to the top of the churn. The lumps were skimmed off the top and placed in a bowl or crock. The butter was then set in the cool water of a stream or spring to harden.

Wooden butter molds were used to press the hardened butter into shapes. The leftover liquid in the churn was buttermilk. People drank the buttermilk or used it in baking.

- *Give each child a clean baby food jar. Fill each jar about half full of cream (about two tablespoons). Fasten lid securely. Check each child's lid to make sure it is fastened.*
- *Have the children shake their jars until the cream turns to butter. Lumps will separate and then mix together into butter. This takes about 10 minutes.*
- *Pour off the liquid.*
- *Place the butter in the refrigerator until the Holy Club closing.*

Always check for allergies before handling or serving food to your children.

The Village School

Supplies: *alphabet chart and any old primers (or books that show pictures of old primers)*

- *Display a completed hornbook (p. 11).*
- *Display a Bible open to Genesis 1:1.*
- *Display an alphabet chart and any old primers (or books that show pictures of old primers).*

SAY: John and Charles Wesley and all the Wesley children were first taught by their mother, Susanna. She taught the children in the kitchen. Both the boys and the girls began their lessons on their fifth birthday. In one day each child was taught the whole alphabet. Two of Susanna's daughters, Molly and Nancy, were considered slow because it took them a day and a half. The next day Susanna expected the child to start reading the Bible. The children began with Genesis chapter one, verse one. Lessons lasted for six hours a day.

When John was ten, he was sent to London to go to school at Charterhouse. Most families had to pay to send their children to school. John was able to go for free because he was a Gownboy. This meant that he was on a kind of scholarship. At Charterhouse Wesley learned Latin, Greek, and Hebrew. He also developed a love for science. It was hard to be one of the younger boys at the school. The older boys often stole the younger boys' food. John got up every morning at 5:00 a.m. and started his day by running around the school garden three times.

Wealthy families hired tutors to teach their children. The tutor was a man who lived with the family. Boys sometimes went on to boarding schools, like the one John Wesley attended.

Girls were given a different kind of education. They were taught how to sew, play musical instruments, and dance. They were also taught how to take care of a home.

Some children became apprentices. An apprentice learned a trade like printing or hatmaking. Apprentices usually lived with the family while they learned.

Children of poor families did not go to school. They often started working at the age of five. These children worked long hours. Some children died from the harsh conditions. John Wesley worked to have free education for all children.

✦ Make Hornbooks

Supplies: *pp 20-21, wood, woodworking tools, sandpaper, clear adhesive paper, glue*

- *Photocopy the hornbook pattern (p. 20)*
- *Cut a hornbook out of wood for each child.*
- *Cut clear adhesive paper to fit the hornbooks.*
- *Photocopy the lesson sheet (p. 21) for each child.*

SAY: Parents often used a hornbook to teach their children to read. Hornbooks were not books. They were wooden boards cut in the shape of paddles. A lesson sheet with the alphabet and the Lord's Prayer was placed on the wooden board. A thin piece of horn covered the lesson sheet. Horn is the translucent outer covering found on the horns of cattle and other animals.

- *Give each child a hornbook. Let the children sand the hornbook with fine sandpaper.*
- *Give each child a lesson sheet. Have the children glue the lesson sheet onto their hornbooks.*
- *Help the children cover the lesson sheets on their hornbooks with clear adhesive paper.*

The Toy Shoppe

Supplies: *handmade or antique toys (dolls, tin soldiers, wooden tops, child's tea set, or marbles)*

- *Display any handmade or antique toys (dolls, tin soldiers, wooden tops, child's tea set, or marbles) you have available.*

SAY: Toys for children were usually homemade. Some wealthy families did buy toys for their children from a toy maker. A wealthy girl might have a fashion doll or a china tea set; a wealthy boy might have a set of tin soldiers.

Homemade toys included cornhusk dolls or rag dolls, kites, tops, jump ropes, and rolling hoops. Children also liked to play with marbles and blow soap bubbles.

On Sunday children were only allowed to play with toys that helped them learn Bible stories. One of the most popular Sunday toys was Noah's ark. This was a wooden boat with a set of wooden animals—in twos, of course!

✦ *Thaumatropes*

Supplies: *p. 22, 4-by-6 cards or posterboard, glue, yarn or string, paper punch*

SAY: The word *thaumatrope* comes from two Greek words that mean "wonder" and "to turn." The toy has two pictures back to back. When the pictures are spun, they look like they become one picture.

Preparation

- *Photocopy the thaumatrope pictures (p. 22) for each child.*
- *Provide 4-by-6 cards. Or cut posterboard into 4-by-6 rectangles. You will need one rectangle for each child.*
- *Cut yarn or string into 14- to 15-inch lengths. You will need two lengths for each child.*

- *Give each child the thaumatrope pictures. Have the children cut out the pictures along the solid lines of the rectangles.*

- *Give each child an index card or posterboard rectangle. Have the children glue the pictures of the horse on one side of the cards or boards. Have the children turn the cards or boards over. Show the children how to glue the pictures of the circuit rider on this side of the cards or boards. The circuit rider pictures should be upside down from the pictures of the horse. Let the glue dry.*

- *Use a paper punch to make a hole in each side of the cards or boards. Give each child two yarn or string pieces. Help the children thread yarn or string through each hole and tie the ends together to make a loop.*

- *Show the children how to wind up the yarn or string and then twirl the cards or boards. The circuit rider will look like he is riding the horse.*

The Wesley Home

Supplies: *Bible, desk and chair, rocker, kitchen table, quill pen (feather), candle, teapot and cups*

- *Set up a large group area for storytelling and drama. The area should be placed where there is room for all the children to hear the story at one time.*

- *Set up a desk and chair, rocker, and kitchen table for Sessions 1-3.*

- *Display a quill pen (feather) and candle on the desk and a teapot and cups on the table.*

The Singing School

Supplies: *p. 17*

- *Have a volunteer dress up as Charles Wesley to lead "The Singing School."*

- *Have the Holy Clubs move to The Wesley Home area and sit down.*

- *Photocopy "How to Sing" (p. 17) to use as a poster.*

SAY: Charles and John Wesley used music to help teach about the Christian faith. Charles wrote over 5,000 hymns. Many of these hymns are in the hymnbook we use in church. John Wesley published four hymnbooks himself. He used many of Charles' hymns in his books.

- *Show the poster, and read the directions to the children.*

✦ Be Present at Our Table, Lord

Supplies: *pp. 18-19*

- *Teach the children "Be Present at Our Table, Lord." (p. 18).*

SAY: The song is traditionally called "The Wesley Grace," although it was not written by John or Charles Wesley. It was named "The Wesley Grace" because of a story that said the words to the song were painted on a teapot used by John.

- *After the children are familiar with the song, teach the children signs for the song in American Sign Language (p. 19).*

SAY: We'll sing and sign this song as a blessing for snack time.

Meet Susanna Wesley

Supplies: *p. 23, costume for Susanna Wesley*

- *Recruit a woman to play the part of Susanna Wesley. Have the woman dress in a costume including a long dress or skirt, a bonnet, and a shawl.*
- *Give the woman the script for Susanna (p. 23). Ask the woman to use the script as a guideline and tell the story in her own words.*

Hear the Bible Story

Supplies: *p. 24, costume for Susanna Wesley*

- *Give the woman the script for the Bible story Susanna is to tell (p. 24).*
- *Have Susanna hold the Bible as she tells the Bible story, "An Answered Prayer."*

Fire!

Supplies: *pp. 25-26, blankets, a wooden box, optional: nightgowns, night shirts, apron, and cap for nurse*

- *Photocopy "Fire!" (pp. 25-26) for the actors.*
- *Choose confident readers for narrator, nurse, John, Mr. Wesley, Mrs. Wesley, Neighbor #1, and Neighbor #2. Let nonreaders play the other Wesley children and make crepe paper flames.*
- *Have the actors present the play for the rest of the children.*

The Holy Clubs

Supplies: *pp. 18-19, butter made earlier (p. 10), crackers, hand-washing supplies, napkins, plastic knives*

- *Have the children wash their hands and then return to their Holy Clubs.*
- *Sing "Be Present at Our Table, Lord."*
- *Serve the butter made at the Village Inn. Let the children use plastic knives to spread the butter on crackers.*

PRAY: Thank you, God, for people throughout history who taught others about your love. Amen.

Always check for allergies before handling or serving food to your children.

Holy Club

Charles Wesley

John Wesley

I will:

- **Get Up Early**

- **Read the Bible**

- **Pray**

- **Not Waste Time**

NAME	Has a Pet	Has a Sister	Has a Brother	Likes to Read	Plays Sports	Likes to Swim	Likes to Dance

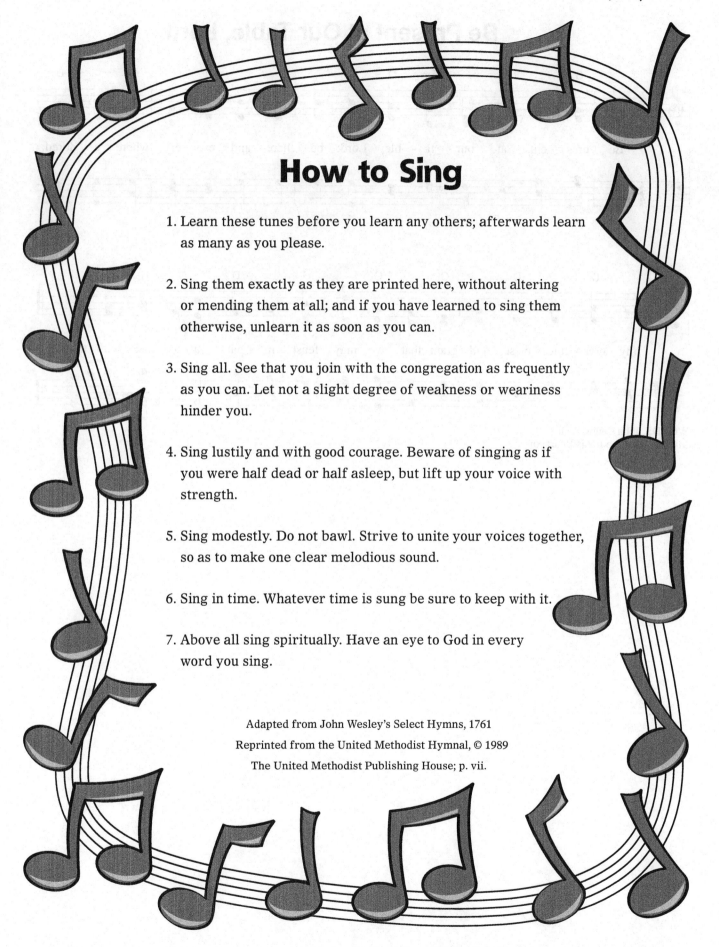

How to Sing

1. Learn these tunes before you learn any others; afterwards learn as many as you please.

2. Sing them exactly as they are printed here, without altering or mending them at all; and if you have learned to sing them otherwise, unlearn it as soon as you can.

3. Sing all. See that you join with the congregation as frequently as you can. Let not a slight degree of weakness or weariness hinder you.

4. Sing lustily and with good courage. Beware of singing as if you were half dead or half asleep, but lift up your voice with strength.

5. Sing modestly. Do not bawl. Strive to unite your voices together, so as to make one clear melodious sound.

6. Sing in time. Whatever time is sung be sure to keep with it.

7. Above all sing spiritually. Have an eye to God in every word you sing.

Adapted from John Wesley's Select Hymns, 1761

Reprinted from the United Methodist Hymnal, © 1989

The United Methodist Publishing House; p. vii.

Be Present at Our Table, Lord

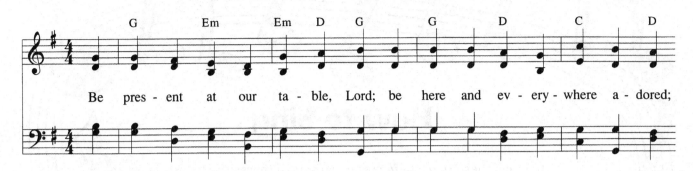

Be pres - ent at our ta - ble, Lord; be here and ev - ery - where a - dored;

thy crea - tures bless, and grant that we may feast in par - a - dise with thee.

WORDS: John Cennick, alt.
MUSIC: Attr. to Louis Bourgeois

Be   present at our   table,   Lord;

Be   here   and everywhere adored;

thy   creatures   bless,

that we   may feast   in paradise

with thee.

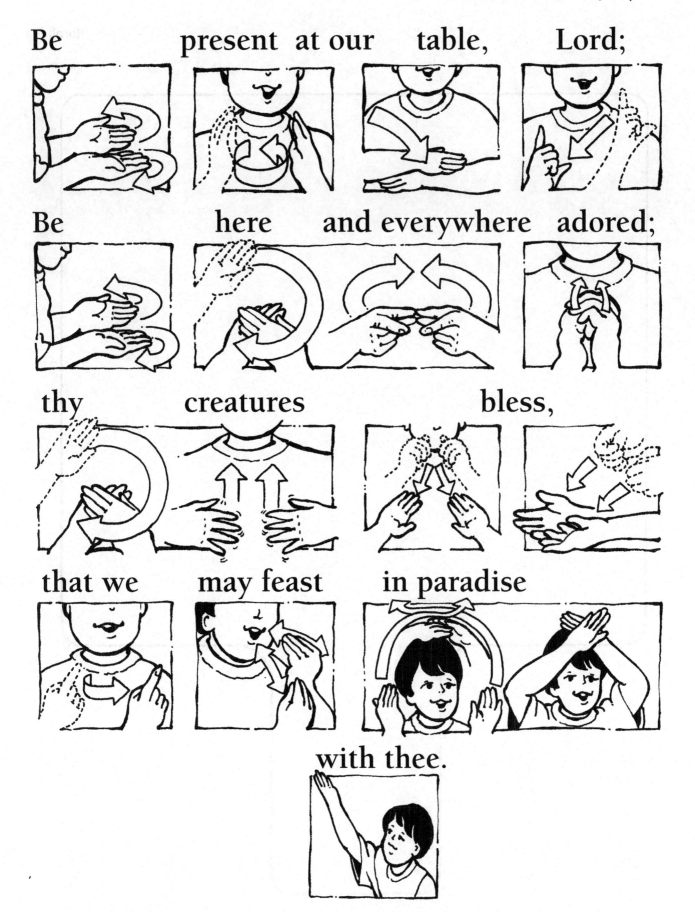

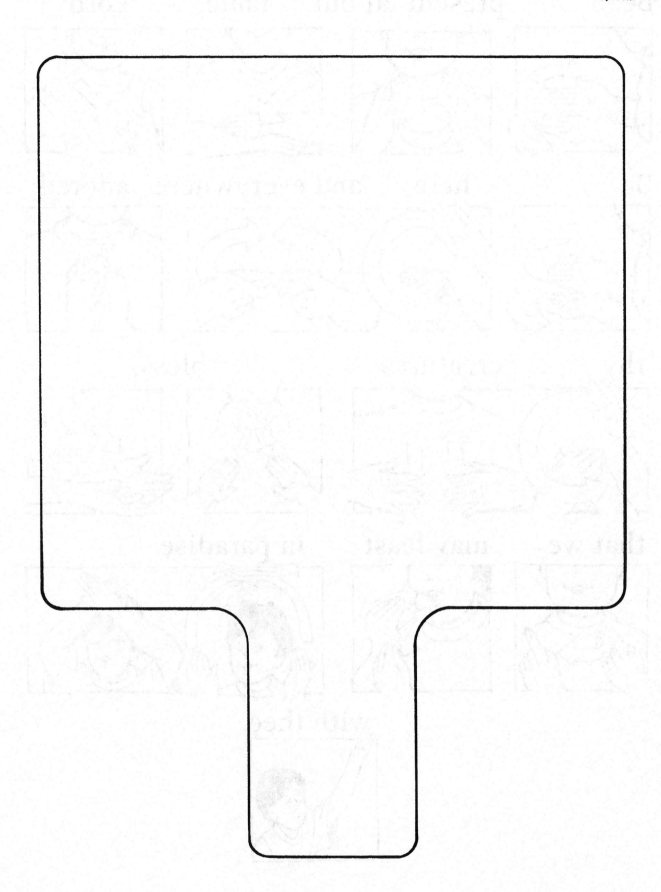

Hornbook

A B C D E F G H I J K L M N O P Q R S T U V W X Y Z

a b c d e f g h i j k l m n o p q r s t u v w x y z

I II III IV V VI VII VIII IX X

Our Father, who art in heaven, hallowed be thy name.

Thy kingdom come, thy will be done

on earth as it is in heaven.

Give us this day our daily bread.

And forgive us our trespasses,

as we forgive those who trespass against us.

And lead us not into temptation, but deliver us from evil.

For thine is the kingdom, and the power,

and the glory, forever. Amen.

From The Ritual of the Former Methodist Church, The United Methodist Hymnal;
© 1989 The United Methodist Publishing House; 895.

Susanna Wesley

Susanna Wesley

I'm Susanna Wesley. My father used to call me Sukey. I was named for a woman in the Bible named Susanna. She was one of the women who helped Jesus and his disciples. I am the youngest of twenty-five children. Can you imagine having twenty-four brothers and sisters? When I grew up, I married a man named Samuel Wesley. He was a pastor in the Church of England. We had nineteen children, but only ten of the nineteen children lived. You may have heard of two of my sons, John and Charles.

The first thing I taught each baby was to cry softly. I spent one hour every week teaching each of my children. On each child's fifth birthday I taught the child the alphabet. The next day I taught that child to read the Bible. We began with the first chapter of Genesis. Repeat the verse after me, "In the beginning, when God created the heavens and the earth" (Genesis 1:1).

Very good. I think that reading the Bible is so important! I loved to gather my children around me and tell them stories from the Bible. They especially liked to hear stories about children. Listen while I tell you one of my children's favorite Bible stories.

An Answered Prayer   by LeeDell Stickler

Once, a long time ago in Bible times, there lived a woman named Hannah and a man named Elkanah (el-KAY-na). They were husband and wife. Hannah and Elkanah loved each other very much and were very happy—except for one thing. They did not have a child to love and care for.

Every year at a special time, Elkanah and Hannah would travel to the temple to worship God. Every year Elkanah and Hannah would say special prayers and make special offerings to God. One of the things they would ask God for was a child to love and care for. And every year they would sadly return to their home. No child would come.

One year Hannah felt especially sad. She prayed very hard, "O God, I am your servant. If you will give me a child to love and care for, then I will dedicate this child to you. I will raise this child to be your servant." Over and over Hannah silently prayed her prayer. She prayed so hard and so long that she moved her lips, but no sound came out.

As she knelt there, Eli, the priest, came into the Temple and saw her. He was upset with what he saw. Here was a woman praying but making no sound. This was embarrassing. "Woman," he said, "you are making a spectacle of yourself! Get up and be on your way!" Eli scolded her.

But Hannah would not give up. "Oh, please sir, do not make me go. There is nothing wrong with me. I am just a woman who is deeply troubled. I am pouring my heart out to God."

Eli felt sorry for Hannah. He wondered what troubled her so. She looked so sad. "Go in peace. May God grant you your prayer."

The next day Hannah and Elkanah went back to their home. Instead of being sad, Hannah was happy. She knew that God had heard her and would answer her prayer. She knew that soon she and Elkanah would have a child to love and care for.

Sure enough, the very next year when it came time to travel to the Temple to worship, Hannah could not go. She had a new baby. The baby's name was Samuel.

At that point in the story John always says, "Samuel, just like Papa!"

"Yes, John, just like your papa."

"Go to the Temple without me," Hannah told her husband, "As soon as Samuel is old enough, I will take him to the Temple just as I promised God."

Four years passed quickly, and the time came for Hannah to keep her promise. She took Samuel to the house of the Lord. She presented Samuel to Eli the priest. "Do you remember me?" she asked Eli. "I am the woman in the Temple who prayed without making a sound. This is the child I asked of God. Now I am keeping my promise. As long as this child lives, he belongs to God."

Samuel helped Eli at the Temple. He filled the lights with oil. He opened and closed the doors. And every year Hannah brought her son a new robe to wear. Hannah and Elkanah had many children. With the birth of each child, Hannah rejoiced and gave thanks to God, just as she had when Samuel was born. Just as I did when John was born, and when Charles was born, and when each of my children was born. Every child is a special gift from God.

(Based on 1 Samuel 1:1-28.)

Fire   by LeeDell Stickler

Characters:

Narrator	Wesley Children (as many as needed)
Nurse	Neighbor 1
John Wesley	Neighbor 2
Mrs. Wesley	Mr. Wesley

Scene 1: Night inside the little cottage

Set: Line several blankets up in a row to be beds. Optional: Girls are wearing long nightgowns. Boys will be wearing night shirts. These could be adult men's shirts. Nurse wears an apron over her dress and a cap.

Narrator: In England, in the little town of Epworth, there lived a family called Wesley. Samuel Wesley was the pastor at a small church in the village. Susanna Wesley was his wife. There were eight Wesley children living at that time. The Wesleys were not a wealthy family; in fact, they were very poor. As a pastor in a local church, Samuel Wesley depended on the people of the village to provide for him and his family. Many of the people from the farms surrounding Epworth did not like to have a preacher in the village. They did not want to help provide for them. In fact, they disliked the pastor so much that sometimes they burned his crops or stole his cattle. This made life very difficult, but the Wesley family did the best they could.

Nurse: (tucking covers around each of the children) Good night. Sleep well, children. God keep you through the night. *(Nurse exits.)*

Narrator: All the Wesley children went to sleep, but everything was not well. Sometime during the middle of the night, a terrible thing happened. The Epworth cottage caught fire. Did some unhappy villager set fire to the house? No one knows exactly how it happened. But sometime during the night, smoke filled the little cottage. Flames licked through the walls. The nursery that was located on the top floor just beneath the thatch roof began to fill with smoke and grew very, very warm.

Nurse: (rushing into the room) Wake up, children! You must not delay!

Wesley children: (rubbing their eyes and sitting up in bed sleepily) What is happening? Why are you getting us up so early?

Nurse: Hurry, the house is on fire! *(The nurse shakes each child. All the children get up but John, who lies back down, pulls the covers over his head, and goes back to sleep.)* Hurry, hurry, hurry. Follow me! *(Nurse leads all the children out of the nursery except John.)*

John: (John sits up and rubs his eyes and calls out.) Nurse! Nurse!

Narrator: John waited for someone to answer. But there was no one to answer. The nurse and all the rest of the children had gone down the steep stairs and out of the house.

John: (now wide awake) What's going on? What is that smell? (cough, cough) It is awfully hot in here. My head hurts. *(John looks around and sees that he is all alone.)* Where is everyone?

Narrator: John realized that he was all alone. He became very frightened. He lept out of bed and rushed to the door of the nursery. But there were flames everywhere. He quickly closed the door and rushed to the window.

John: Help! Help! The house is on fire! *(rushes to the window and tries to push it open)* Open, open, open! I've got to get the window open! *(at last the window opens and John leans out)*

Scene 2: Outside the Epworth cottage

Give nonreaders red crepe paper streamers. Have John stand on a wooden box. Let the younger children sit on the floor around John's box and wave crepe paper streamers for flames.

Narrator: When John looked down on the garden below him, he could see a group of neighbors. They were crying and shouting and running about. Some were carrying leather buckets filled with water.

Mr. Wesley: (touching each child's head as he counts) One, two, three, four, five, six, seven…Susanna, I do not see John!

Mrs. Wesley: (grabbing the nurse by the arm) Where is John?

Nurse: (trembling) I woke the girls up when I heard Hetty screaming. I picked up the baby and called to John to come. I thought he was right behind me! He must have stayed behind. (Nurse falls to her knees and begins to pray.) Dear God, you have to save John.

Mrs. Wesley: John must still be in the house. I must go to him. I am sure he is frightened to death. (starts to run back into the cottage but is stopped by the two neighbors)

Neighbor #1: You can't go in there. Everything is on fire. You will be killed.

Neighbor #2: The roof is on fire. It will fall down very soon.

Mrs. Wesley: But my son is still in there. I have to save John!

Narrator: The fire was spreading. Large pieces of the burning thatch fell to the ground around the people who were standing outside.

Neighbor #2: Look up there! In the window just below the roof. Is that not John?

Mr. Wesley: It is John! He's in the nursery. Thank God, he is still alive!

Narrator: Mr. Wesley tried to reach up to John, but the window was just too high.

Mr. Wesley: (dropping to his knees to pray) Dear God, help us, please. We must save John.

Neighbor #1: I've got an idea. Come! (gestures to neighbor standing nearby) Get on my shoulders. Then we will be tall enough to reach the boy.

Narrator: The neighbor stooped over and let the other man climb on his shoulders. (Do not allow the children to stand on each other's shoulders. Have the two neighbors stand side by side and reach up for John.) The first time he fell over. But on the second try, he stood up straight and tall. Between the two of them, they were exactly the right height.

Neighbor #2: Here, John, lean out a little farther. I will catch you.

Narrator: John crawled into the window and leaned out—farther, farther, farther. By now the flames were practically on his nightshirt. John was frightened. He could not go back in, but he was afraid to climb out.

Mrs. Wesley: Climb out, John. Climb out!

Narrator: The neighbor reached out for John and grasped him under the arms. He lifted him from the burning house and lowered him safely into the hands of the people below. Almost as soon as John was on the ground, the roof collapsed.

Mrs. Wesley: (hugging John) Thank God! You are safe!

Mr. Wesley: Come neighbors, let us thank God! John has been snatched as a brand from the burning. God has given me all my children. Do not worry about the house. All my family is safe. I am rich enough.

Narrator: All the neighbors dropped to their knees with the Wesley family and gave thanks to God.

The End

Session 2: John Wesley

In this session your children will learn more about John Wesley. John Wesley became a clergyman in the Church of England, but John felt like he had fallen short of what God wanted him to do. One night he went to a Bible study at a meeting on Aldersgate Street in London. At that meeting, John said, "I felt my heart strangely warmed."

Suggestions for Session 2

1. *Begin the Session in the Holy Clubs and play jack straws with the children.*
2. *Move to The Village Shoppes.*
3. *Choose all or some of the following shoppes:*
   The Village Inn: Make Drop Biscuits
   The Tannery: Make Saddlebags
   The Silversmith: Silver Symbols
4. *Gather the children into a large group for the activities in The Wesley Home.*
5. *Send the children back to their Holy Clubs to enjoy their snacks and close the session.*

Volunteers Needed

- *Holy Club Leaders*
- *Shoppe Leaders: The Village Inn, The Tannery, The Silversmith*
- *Charles Wesley*
- *John Wesley*
- *Actors for "The Barefoot Preacher"*

Holy Clubs
Meet With the Holy Clubs

Supplies: *p. 15, quilts, can with sand or gravel, dowel or stick*

- *Place quilts on the floor to designate each Holy Club.*
- *Photocopy the "Holy Club" sign (p. 15) for each club.*
- *Make one saddlebag for each Holy Club (pp. 30-31).*
- *Give the children their nametags.*

✦ Jack Straws

Supplies: *pickup sticks*

- *Let the children play "Pickup Sticks," the modern-day version of "Jack Straws."*

SAY: "Jack Straws" was a game played with pieces of straw. Children made a small pile with the straws. Each child took a turn trying to pull a straw from the pile without moving any other straw. If the child was successful, he or she made one point. The children took turns until the pile of straws fell over. The child with the most points was the winner.

Involve the children in the game as soon as they arrive.

✦ Tell About John Wesley

SAY: John Wesley became a clergyman in the Church of England. But John began to question his faith. He felt like he had fallen short of what God wanted him to do.

One night he went to a Bible study at a meeting on Aldersgate Street in London. At that meeting, John said, "I felt my heart strangely warmed." He felt God's love. He felt that God was sending him to tell everyone about God's love.

John began preaching outside of the churches. Many people came to hear him preach, especially the people who were poor. John started riding his horse from place to place.

He preached two or three times every day, seven days a week. He carried a saddlebag with books and food. He preached in fields, in mines, and near factories. John Wesley felt that the world was his parish.

✦ Missions

- *Tell the children about any mission project your group is doing as part of Journey With J.W.*

✦ Learn the Bible Verse

Supplies: *Bible, saddlebag*

Then I heard the Lord's voice saying,

"Whom should I send, and who will go for us?"

I said, "I'm here; send me!"

Isaiah 6:8

- *Choose a child to read the verse from the Bible.*
- *Have the children sit in a circle. Give the child sitting next to you a saddlebag. Have the child put the saddlebag behind his or her back.*
- *Have the children pass the saddlebag around the circle behind their backs.*
- *Say: "Stop!" Have the child holding the saddlebag when you say "stop" repeat the Bible verse. Continue playing the game until each child has been caught with the saddlebag and has quoted the Bible verse.*

Make a saddlebag (pp. 30-31) for each Holy Club.

✦ *Repeat Matthew 28:19*

- Repeat "Therefore, go and make disciples of all nations" (Matthew 28:19) with the children

The Village Shoppes

The Village Inn

Supplies: *baskets, wooden bowls, iron skillets, teapots, and churns*

- Use the Village Inn set up from Session 1.

✦ *Make Drop Biscuits*

Supplies: *ingredients for drop biscuits, mixing bowl, measuring cups and spoons, baking sheets, tablespoons and forks*

- Have the children wash their hands.
- Use the recipe below with the children.

Colonial Drop Biscuits

2 cups flour	1 tbs. baking powder
¼ tsp. salt	2 eggs
¾ cup heavy cream	

- Preheat oven to 400 degrees.
- Have the children measure the flour, salt, and baking powder into a large bowl. Mix together.
- Beat eggs and add to mixture.
- Add cream and stir with a fork. Batter will be lumpy.
- Show the children how to use a tablespoon to drop the batter onto the baking sheet.
- Bake 15 minutes. Makes 24 small biscuits.
- Save the biscuits until the Holy Club closing.

Always check for allergies before handling or serving food to your children.

The Tannery

Supplies: *leather items such as belts, hats, shoes or boots, coats, wallets, Optional: saddlebags and saddle*

- *Display leather items that you have available such as leather belts, hats, and shoes or boots. If possible, display a leather saddle and saddlebags.*

SAY: The tannery was the name of the shop where leather was made from tanning animal skins. Tanning made the skins soft and easy to bend. It also helped waterproof the leather. During the late 1700s most leather workers used vegetable matter and tree bark to tan animal skins. The skins were placed out in the sun to dry. Bark from trees like oak and hemlock was mixed with water in large pots called vats. After the skins were dry, they were put in the vats to soak for several weeks. The mixture in the vats smelled bad, but it softened the skins so they could be cut and sewn into things like shoes, clothing, saddles, and saddlebags.

✦ Make Saddlebags

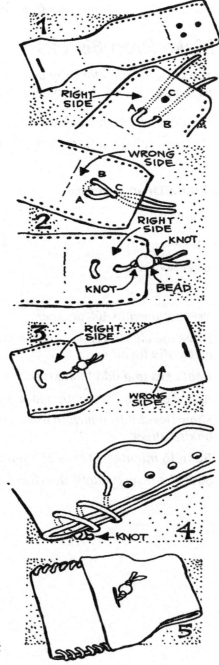

Make one saddlebag for each *Holy Club* to use in opening session.

Supplies: *pp. 36-37, 7-by-17-inch rectangle of vinyl per saddlebag, ¾-inch bead per saddlebag, three 15-inch pieces of plastic lacing per saddlebag, paper punch or leather punch, scissors, pen, self-sealing plastic bags*

- *Photocopy the saddlebag pattern (pp. 36-37). Cut out the pattern and punch out the holes.*

- *Use a pen to trace the saddlebag pattern onto the wrong side of the vinyl and mark the holes.*

- *Cut out the vinyl. Punch out holes. If you do not have a leather punch, use scissors to clip the three holes in the center of the bottom part of the bag (A, B, and C). A paper punch will not reach these holes.*

- *Cut plastic lacing into three 15-inch pieces for each saddlebag.*

- *Set out one bead for each saddlebag.*

- *Place enough beads, lacing pieces, and vinyl pieces together inside a self-sealing plastic bag for the number of children in each Holy Club.*

- *Give each child a vinyl piece and the three plastic lacing pieces. Start with one plastic lacing piece. Have the children turn the saddlebag to the right side. Show the children how to thread one end of the plastic lacing through hole A and the other end of the plastic lacing through hole B.*

- *Turn the saddlebag to the wrong side. Thread both ends of the plastic lacing back through hole C. The ends should now be showing on the right side of the vinyl. Tie the ends of the plastic lacing together about 1-inch below hole C. Give each child a bead. Have each child thread the bead over the two ends of the plastic lacing to rest against the knot. Tie another knot in the plastic lacing to secure the bead.*

- *Turn the vinyl so that the wrong side is up. Fold up the bottom part (the section with the three holes and bead) of the saddlebag so that the holes on each side match. The bead should now be facing up.*

- *Have the children knot one end of one of the remaining pieces of plastic lacing. Show the children how to sew one side of the saddlebag together using an overcast stitch. Tie off the ends of the plastic lacing, and weave the end back through the stitches. Repeat on the second side.*

The Silversmith

Supplies: *old medicine bottles*

- *Display items made of silver, pewter, or tin, such as teapots, bowls, candle holders, pitchers, or mugs.*

SAY: John Wesley was sent to school at Charterhouse and then at Oxford University. However, school was not available for all children like it is today. Many poor children started working when they were five. Children became apprentices in order to learn a skill or trade. A child might become an apprentice with a wig maker, leather worker, needle worker, or silversmith. Sometimes the apprentice was taught how to read and write. The apprentice often lived with the shopkeeper's family for several years to learn the trade.

Silver is a very soft metal. The silversmith would melt the silver and add other metals, such as copper, to make the silver stronger. In England there were rules that told the silversmiths how much of the other metals they were allowed to add. Silver that contained ninety-two percent pure silver was called sterling. This meant that the silver was of good quality.

After the silversmiths melted the silver, they cast it into a solid sheet of metal. The sheet was then cut and hammered into whatever the silversmith was making. Some of the things silversmiths made were bowls, pitchers, teapots, silverware, trays, mugs, or porringers. (A porringer was a shallow bowl.)

The silversmith would have to keep heating the piece of silver to make it easy to bend. When the piece was finished, the silversmith would polish it in order to get rid of any hammer marks and make the piece shine. Sometimes the silversmith would make designs or pictures on the piece.

Silversmiths often melted down silver coins people had saved and used the silver to make other silver things, such as teapots. The teapot had the same value as the coins. A famous silversmith in colonial America was Paul Revere.

♦ *Silver Symbols*

Supplies: *p. 42; cardboard, posterboard, or plastic lids; aluminum foil; yarn; glue; shallow trays; washable paint; paintbrushes; paper towels or tissues; paper punch*

- *Cut cardboard or posterboard into 4-inch circles or squares. Or provide plastic lids from peanut cans, potato chip cans, or powdered drink cans.*

- *Cut aluminum foil into 6-inch squares.*

- *Cut yarn into two 8-inch pieces.*

- *Photocopy the symbol poster (p. 42).*

- *Give each child a cardboard or posterboard circle or square or a plastic lid.*

- *Show the children the symbol poster (p. 42). Talk to the children about the symbols.*

- *Pour glue into shallow trays. Give each child a piece of yarn. Have the children dip the yarn into the glue and then use the yarn to make a simple Christian symbol on the board or lid. Let the glue set for a few minutes.*

- *Give each child a square of aluminum foil. Show the children how to lay the foil over the yarn, covering the lid completely and wrapping the excess foil underneath the board or lid. Have the children press the foil around the edge inside the lid and over the yarn so that an impression of the symbol shows.*

- *Let the children use paintbrushes to brush washable paint over the foil symbol. Immediately have the children use paper towels or tissues to wipe off all the paint. This will give the foil symbol an antique look.*

- *Use a paper punch to punch a hole in the top of each foil symbol. Tie the second piece of yarn through the hole to make a hanger.*

The Wesley Home

Supplies: *Bible, desk and chair, rocker, kitchen table, quill pen (feather), candle, teapot and cups*

- *Continue to use the Wesley Home set up in Session 1.*

The Singing School

Supplies: *pp. 34-35*

- *Have the Holy Clubs move to The Wesley Home area and sit down.*

- *Teach the children three hymns written by Charles Wesley.*

"O For a Thousand Tongues to Sing"
(page 34; The United Methodist Hymnal #57)

"Hark! the Herald Angels Sing"
(page 35; The United Methodist Hymnal #240)

"A Charge to Keep I Have"
(page 34; The United Methodist Hymnal #413)

Meet John Wesley

Supplies: *p. 38, costume for John Wesley*

- *Recruit a man to pretend to be John Wesley. Have the man dress in a costume including knee breeches and a tail coat. Or have the man wear a black ministerial robe.*
- *John Wesley let his hair grow long to save the money he would have to spend on hair cuts, so the man pretending to be John might wear a wig if he does not have long hair.*
- *Ask the man to use the script (p. 38) as a guideline and tell the story in his own words.*

Hear the Bible Story

Supplies: *p. 39, costume for John Wesley*

- *Give the man the script for the Bible story John is to tell (p. 39).*
- *Have John hold the Bible as he tells the Bible story, "A Good Heart."*

The Barefoot Preacher

Supplies: *pp. 40-41, table and chair, Optional: long skirts for girls, tricorn hats for boys*

- *Photocopy "The Barefoot Preacher!" (pp. 40-41) for the actors.*
- *Choose confident readers for narrator, John Wesley, Charles Delamotte, James and Caroline, Ruth and Stephen. Let nonreaders play the children at Sunday school.*
- *Have the actors present the play to the children.*

The Holy Clubs

Supplies: *p. 18, biscuits made earlier (p. 29), honey, hand-washing supplies, napkins, plastic spoons*

- *Have the children wash their hands and then return to their Holy Clubs.*
- *Sing "Be Present at Our Table, Lord."*
- *Let the children add honey to their biscuits and eat.*

PRAY: Thank you, God, for people throughout history who taught others about your love. Amen.

Always check for allergies before handling or serving food to your children.

O For a Thousand Tongues to Sing

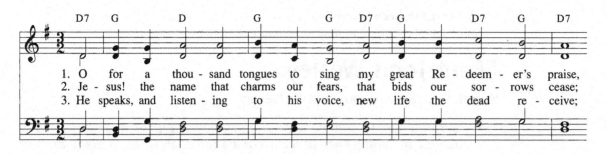

WORDS: Charles Wesley
MUSIC: Carl G. Gläser; arr. by Lowell Mason

A Charge to Keep I Have

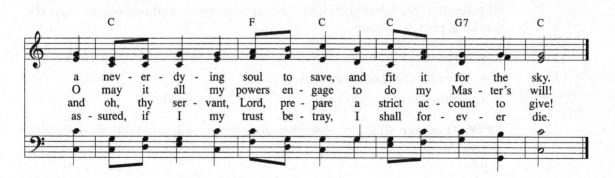

WORDS: Charles Wesley
MUSIC: Lowell Mason

Hark! the Herald Angels Sing

WORDS: Charles Wesley; alt. by George Whitefield and others
MUSIC: Felix Mendelssohn; arr. by William H. Cummings

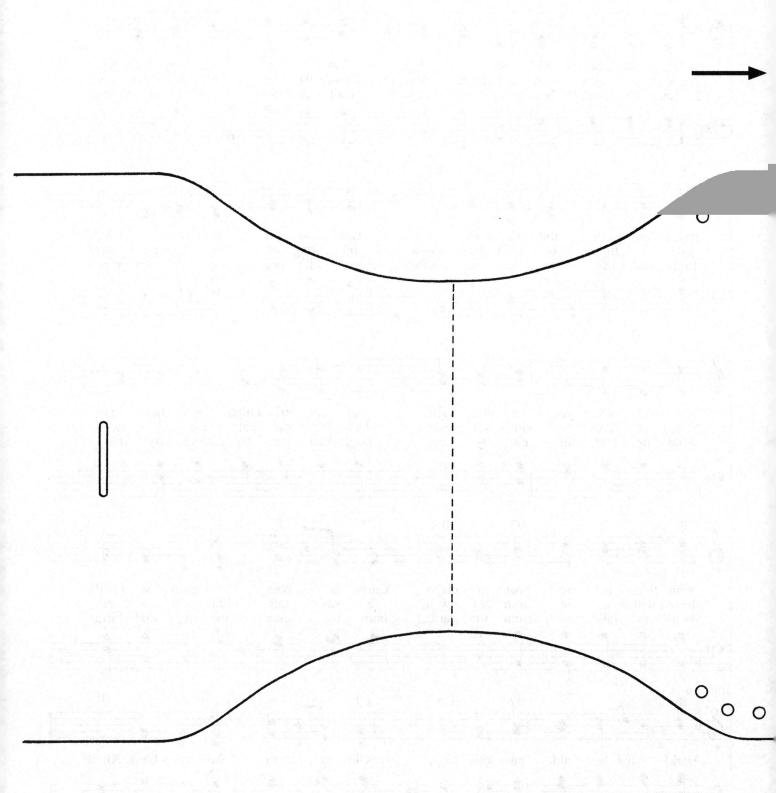

Tape pattern together so that arrows align.

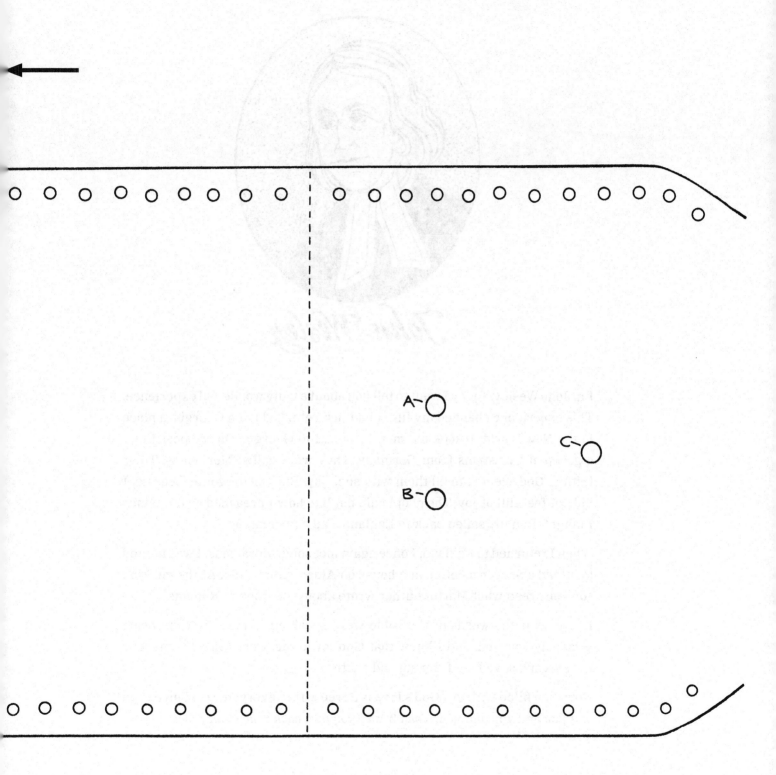

John Wesley by Pam Buchholz

I'm John Wesley. Today I want to tell you about a truly wonderful experience. This experience changed my life. I had just returned from Georgia, a place in the New World. It took me months to sail to Georgia. On the boat I met a group of Christians from Germany. They were called Moravians. Their faith in God seemed to fill them with such joy. But when I got to Georgia, I did not feel full of joy. The people did not like how I preached or the things I taught. I finally sailed back to England, sad and unhappy.

When I returned to England, I once again met some Moravians. I was invited to attend a prayer meeting at a house on Aldersgate Street. At the meeting someone read what Martin Luther wrote about the Book of Romans.

It was as if the words of the Bible were speaking to me. I felt my heart strangely warmed, and I knew that God loved me. Christ had taken away my sins and saved me from sin and death.

Now I am filled with joy. God's love is a free gift to everyone. God loves you and you and you and you. *(John Wesley points at each child in the group.)*

A Good Heart by LeeDell Stickler

Did you know that my father's name was Samuel? My father loved God very much and served God by preaching and helping others. There is a Samuel in the Bible, too. The Samuel in the Bible was a judge. The land of Israel was ruled by judges instead of kings. These judges talked with God, and God helped them decide what was right for the people. But the people looked around at the other countries. All the other countries had kings. They wanted to be like the other countries, so they came to their judge, Samuel.

"Samuel, instead of a judge, we want a king. All the other countries around us have kings. We want one, too," the people complained.

Samuel tried to change their mind. But still they wanted a king. Samuel told God what the people had said.

"Why do my people want a king?" God asked Samuel. "I am their ruler."

But still the people complained and complained. Finally, God chose Saul to be the first king.

At first Saul did everything that God told him to do. He talked with God and asked God what was the right thing to do. But as time went on, Saul began to feel more and more like a king. He grew too busy to talk to God. Soon, Saul ignored God and what God said to do. God was not pleased with King Saul.

Then one day God said to Samuel, "Saul is a disappointment. He no longer listens to me. I have decided that it is time to choose another king. Fill your horn with oil, and set out for Bethlehem. There you will find Jesse and his family. I will choose one of his sons to be the new king of Israel."

"But what if the king discovers where I am going and why? I will be in big trouble," said Samuel.

"Tell everyone that you are going to Bethlehem to have a special celebration. Invite Jesse and his family to come. While they are there, I will show you which son I have chosen. Saul will not suspect what you are truly about."

And so Samuel set out for Bethlehem. He invited everyone to come to Jesse's house for a special celebration.

Now, everyone was curious as to why Samuel was there. Not only was he a powerful man of God, he was also a special advisor to the king. So everyone hurried to Jesse's house.

Samuel said to Jesse, "I would like to see all of your sons. Have them come before me."

Jesse did not understand why Samuel wanted to see his sons, but he had them come and stand before Samuel, one at a time. Samuel looked at each young man closely, waiting for God to give the word. Each son was tall and strong and handsome. As each stood before Samuel, Samuel thought to himself, *Surely this is the one that God has chosen.*

But God said to Samuel, "Do not look at the appearance. I do not see as people see. I look at a person's heart."

Eight of Jesse's sons came to Samuel. But God did not choose any of them to be the next king. Then Samuel asked Jesse, "Are these your only sons?"

"My youngest is not here. He is in the field keeping the sheep," said Jesse.

"Send for him. We will not sit down to our feast until he comes," said Samuel.

Jesse sent for his son David. When David arrived, Samuel could see that he was as handsome as his brothers, but God saw that David had a good heart. "This is the one that I have chosen," said God. "He will be the next king of Israel. Rise and anoint him with oil."

Then Samuel took the horn of oil and poured it over David's head. From that day forward the Spirit of God was with David—even though it was many years before he actually became the new king.

(Based on 1 Samuel 16:1-13.)

The Barefoot Preacher by LeeDell Stickler

Characters:

Narrator	John Wesley
Charles Delamotte	Children at the Sunday school

James and Caroline *(well-dressed, from wealthy families)*

Ruth and Stephen *(shabbily dressed, from poorer families)*

Scene 1: A cottage in Savannah, Georgia

Set: a crude wooden table with a chair, a candle on the table. Optional: long skirts for the girls, tricorn hats for the boys. Ruth and Stephen should be barefoot.

Narrator: Many years ago before the United States was actually the United States, it was a group of colonies that belonged to England. Many people came to the colonies to clear land for farms and make a new life for themselves. John Wesley dreamed of the time when he could go to the New World and preach the message of Jesus Christ to the people who were there and to the Native Americans who lived there. One day this dream came true. John and his brother Charles came to the colony of Georgia and the small river town of Savannah. But John's dream was not all that he had hoped it would be. John talked about his concerns with his friend, Charles Delamotte.

John Wesley: *(sitting down at a table with his head in his hands)* I just don't understand it. I preach the gospel to the people; I tell them what they are doing wrong. I tell them how to change their ways, but no one is listening. Instead of making people feel closer to Jesus, I am driving them away. What am I doing wrong?

Charles Delamotte: Well, John, I can tell you. You are a young man. Your beliefs are very strong. Many of these people do not want to hear how bad they are. They want to know that God loves them and accepts them just the way they are.

John Wesley: But being a Christian is serious business. They must stop being so frivolous.

Charles Delamotte: John, you need to lighten up.

Narrator: Now, John wanted people to change their ways. And so he kept telling people what they were doing wrong. Many people did not like him. One day John had an idea.

John Wesley: I have always gotten on well with children. Perhaps if the adults will not listen to me, the children will. I will begin a school for children to learn about God and about Jesus.

Narrator: So John Wesley began the first Sunday school in the colony. At first, many children came. Then fewer and fewer children began to show up.

John Wesley: *(scratches head)* I don't understand what happened. At first many children came to our Sunday school. Now, only the wealthy children attend. Why are the poor children staying away?

Charles Delamotte: The poor children are not coming to Sunday school because the rich boys are making fun of them for not wearing shoes.

John Wesley: What a person wears to come to church is not important. God does not care if they are wearing shoes or not. God loves them just the way they are.

Charles Delamotte: Well, some of the children are embarrassed. That is why they are staying away.

John: I've got an idea. Today, I will teach the class! *(John sits down and begins to take off his shoes.)*

Scene 2: At the village church where the boys and girls have come for Sunday school

Set: *wooden benches and a table in the front for the teacher.*

Narrator: That Sunday morning, John Wesley walked calmly toward the church. All along the road the children began to follow and point.

Ruth: *(skipping along behind him)* Look, the Reverend has no shoes on!

Stephen: Did you forget your shoes, Reverend Wesley? Aren't your toes cold?

Caroline: Humph! Surely the pastor is not going into the church without his shoes.

James: How embarrassing for a pastor to be seen without his shoes. It isn't right to be seen at church without the proper clothing!

Narrator: But John Wesley paid no attention to the comments from the people as he walked. And when he got to the church, to everyone's surprise, he walked right in—bare feet and all.

Children: *(whispering and pointing toward John Wesley's bare feet)* Look! Look! The preacher is barefoot!

Narrator: But John Wesley said not a single word. He walked to the front of the group and began the lesson. He paid no attention to the giggling and talking from the girls and boys. He did not even seem to notice that he was barefoot.

Scene 3: Several Sundays later at Sunday school

Set: *same as scene 2*

Narrator: Every Sunday John Wesley appeared with his feet bare. Every Sunday he conducted the lesson as though nothing was different. But soon, something different began to happen. More and more children came to Sunday school.

Stephen: *(who is dressed rather shabbily and is barefoot)* I am not embarrassed to be without shoes if the pastor himself is without shoes.

Ruth: The Reverend says that God had Moses take his shoes off when God spoke to him through the burning bush. If Moses and Reverend Wesley can be without their shoes before God, I suppose it's all right for me.

Narrator: Soon the other boys who had made fun of the children without shoes began to feel ashamed of their cruel behavior.

John Wesley: God loves you just the way you are.

The End

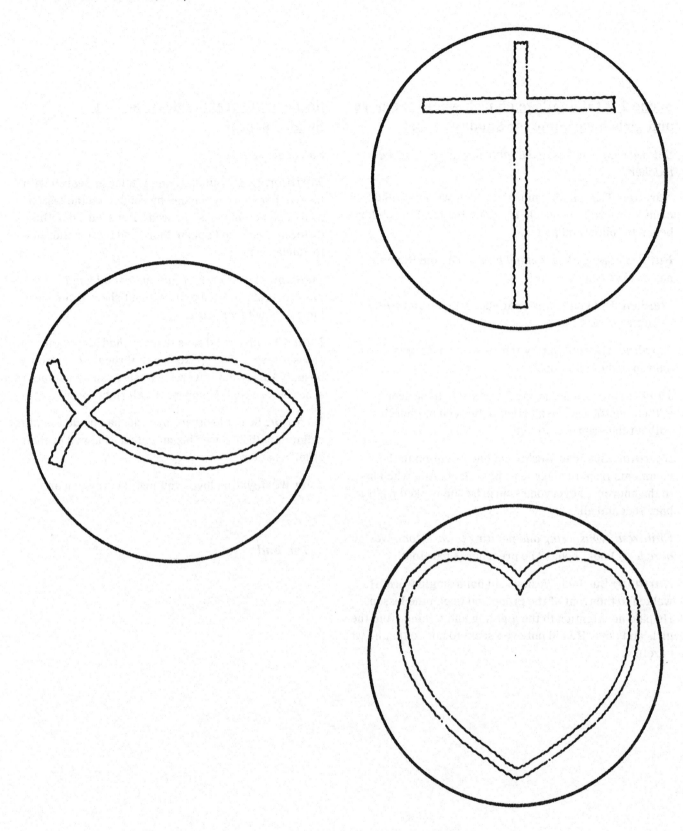

Session 3: Charles Wesley

In this session your children will be introduced to Charles Wesley. Charles was the eighteenth child of Samuel and Susanna Wesley. Charles became a pastor like his father and brother, but he is best known for the many hymns he wrote to teach Scriptures.

Suggestions for Session 3

1. *Begin the Session in the Holy Clubs and play "Going to Jerusalem" with the children.*
2. *Move to The Village Shoppes.*
3. *Choose all or some of the following shoppes:*
   The Village Inn: Make Gingerbread
   The Apothecary: Make Powder
   The Jail: Go to Debtor's Prison, Make Shackles, Visit the Prisoners
4. *Gather the children into a large group for the activities in The Wesley Home.*
5. *Send the children back to their Holy Clubs to enjoy their snacks and close the session.*

Volunteers Needed

- *Holy Club Leaders*
- *Shoppe Leaders: The Village Inn, The Apothecary, The Jail*
- *Charles Wesley*
- *John Wesley*
- *Actors for "The Forgotten Wesley"*

Holy Clubs
Meet With the Holy Clubs

Supplies: *pp. 15 and 50, quilts, can with sand or gravel, dowel or stick*

- *Photocopy the play money (p. 50). Each Holy Club will need money for the jail activity.*
- *Place quilts on the floor to designate each Holy Club.*
- *Photocopy the "Holy Club" sign (p. 15) for each club.*
- *Give the children their nametags.*

◈ *Going to Jerusalem*

Supplies: *p. 18, chairs*

SAY: "Going to Jerusalem" was a game played by children in early America. It was played like musical chairs.

Involve the children in the game as soon as they arrive.

- *Set up enough chairs so that all the children, except one, have a place to sit. Place the chairs in two lines back to back.*
- *Sing "Be Present at Our Table, Lord" (p. 18). Have the children walk around the chairs while you sing.*
- *Stop singing. Have all the children try to sit on a chair. The child left standing is out. Take out another chair and play the game again.*
- *Continue until only one chair and one child is left.*
- *To play a noncompetitive version of this game, take away the chairs but have all the children stay in the game. The children wind up sitting on each others' laps.*

◈ *Tell About the Wesley Brothers*

SAY: John and his brother Charles took the good news about Jesus to people who were not welcome inside the churches. They went to hospitals, workhouses, and prisons.

John was the first person to open a place where poor people could come to get free medicines. He hired a doctor and an apothecary to help people who could not pay for medicines or doctor visits.

John also organized Methodist Societies. These were class meetings or small groups that met to share their faith and help each live as Christians. The Societies usually met in people's homes.

John Wesley taught:

> Do all the good you can,
>
> By all the ways you can,
>
> In all the places you can,
>
> At all the times you can,
>
> To all the people you can,
>
> As long as ever you can.

◈ *Missions*

- *Tell the children about any mission project your group is doing as part of* Journey With J. W.

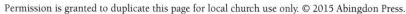

✦ Learn the Bible Verse

Supplies: *Bible, p. 51, scissors*

> "How wonderful is the coming of messengers who bring good news!"
> *Romans 10:15, (GNT)*

- *Choose a child to read the Bible verse from the Bible.*
- *Photocopy the Bible verse cards (p. 51). Cut the cards apart. Scramble the cards and place them in the center of your group. Have each child pick a card from the pile.*
- *Have the children hold their cards and put themselves in order of the Bible verse. Say the Bible verse together.*
- *Continue the game until each child has an opportunity to hold a card.*

✦ Repeat Matthew 28:19

- *Repeat "Therefore, go and make disciples of all nations" (Matthew 28:19) with the children.*

The Village Shoppes

The Village Inn

Supplies: *baskets, wooden bowls, iron skillets, teapots, and churns*

- *Use the Village Inn set up from Session 1.*

✦ Make Gingerbread

Supplies: *gingerbread ingredients, mixing bowls, mixing cups and spoons, cookie sheets, rolling pin*

- *Use the recipe below to prepare dough.*

Gingerbread

1½ cups dark molasses	²/3 cup cold water
1 cup packed brown sugar	¹/3 cup shortening
7 cups flour	2 tsp. baking soda
1 tsp. salt	1 tsp. allspice
1 tsp. nutmeg	1 tsp. cinnamon
raisins	

Always check for allergies before handling or serving food to your children.

JOURNEY
with J.W.

- *Mix brown sugar, water, and shortening in a large bowl.*
- *Mix together and add the remaining ingredients.*
- *Cover and refrigerate for at least two hours.*
- *Heat oven to 350 degrees.*
- *Have the children wash their hands.*
- *Lightly grease cookie sheets.*
- *Lightly flour the work surface.*
- *Give each child a portion of the dough. Show the children how to roll the dough until it is about ¼-inch thick.*
- *Show the children how to use a gingerbread doll-shaped cookie cutter to cut the dough. Help the children place their cookies on the cookie sheet.*
- *Let the children decorate the cookies with raisins.*
- *Bake for 10-12 minutes.*
- *Makes about 42 six-inch gingerbread dolls.*
- *Save the gingerbread to eat in the Holy Clubs.*

The Apothecary

Supplies: *old medicine bottles*

- *Display old medicine bottles.*

SAY: The apothecary was someone who prepared and sold drugs and other medicines. People in Wesley's time did not know a lot about medicine like we do today. They did not know that diseases were spread by germs. People did not take many baths, and they did not wash their clothes very often.

People thought that sickness was caused by bad blood. When someone became sick, many times the doctor would use leeches to bleed the sick person. The leeches sucked blood from the patient. Bleeding often caused the person who was sick to become very weak and even die.

Poultices were made for aches and pains. A poultice was a kind of paste made of herbs. The paste was put on whatever part of the body hurt. Tonics were liquids that were used as medicine. People thought that tonics needed to taste bitter to work.

John Wesley was very interested in medicine. He had many ideas about what to do to keep healthy. He thought that people should get exercise and eat plain foods. If you had a deep cut, Wesley would tell you to bind toasted cheese on the cut. If you were losing your hair, Wesley would suggest rubbing your scalp with honey and onions. Wesley also experimented with electricity as a way to cure many health problems. He thought electric shocks helped the person get better.

Wesley was the first person to open a place where poor people could come to get free medicines. Wesley hired a doctor and an apothecary to help people who could not pay.

✦ Powder

Supplies: *cornstarch; essential oil; fake fur; clean plastic yogurt containers with lids, small chip cans with lids, or small jewelry boxes with lids; floral wrapping paper; scissors*

SAY: **Although John Wesley thought that bathing in cold water was good for your health, most people thought that if they took a bath too often, they would get sick. Many wealthy people used heavy perfumes and powders to make themselves smell better.**

Most men and boys and many women wore wigs. Sometimes the wigs were huge mounds of false hair. Many people powdered the wigs so that the hair looked white.

One box of cornstarch makes a little over 5 jars of powder.

- *Gather clean plastic yogurt containers with lids, small (2 oz.) chip cans with lids, or small jewelry boxes with lids.*
- *Cut floral wrapping paper to fit around the containers.*
- *Cut fake fur into two-inch circles to make powder puffs.*
- *Give each child a small plastic container or jewelry box with a lid and wrapping paper.*
- *Show the children how to glue the wrapping paper around the container or box.*
- *Empty the box of cornstarch into a large bowl.*
- *Add a few drops of essential oil (this is very concentrated).*
- *Let the children mix the oil and cornstarch together.*
- *Encourage the children to smell the mixture.*
- *Place a small amount of powder (about 2-3 ounces) in each container.*
- *Give each child a powder puff to set on top of the powder.*
- *Immediately cover the container with a lid.*
- *Tape the lid closed to send home.*

The Jail

✦ Set Up the Jail

Supplies: *separate room or two large appliance boxes, tape, ribbon, garbage bags, burlap, toy rats*

- *Use a separate room or two large appliance boxes to make the jail.*
- *If you use a separate room, tape ribbon over the doorway to make prison bars. Cover the windows with paper, cloth, or garbage bags to make the room dark.*
- *If you use appliance boxes, open one of the ends of each box and tape them together to make a larger jail. Cut one small window high up on the box as the only window. Cut a door in the side of one of the boxes.*
- *Throw burlap cloth on the floor of the jail.*
- *Have one or two plastic toy rats (dog or cat toys) on the floor.*

◆ Go to Debtor's Prison

- *Have the jailer arrest each Holy Club for not being able to pay their debts. Put half of the club members in the jail. If children want to give the jailer their play money to pay their debts, make the debt more than the amount of money they have. Schedule jail time so that each Holy Club has a turn during the village shoppe time.*

- *Once half of the Holy Club members are arrested, the jailer takes those club members to jail and has them sit down on the floor of the jail. Let the jailer tell the club members about debtor's prison.*

SAY: The condition of jails in the time of the Wesleys was very poor. The jails or prisons were damp, dirty, and often overrun with rats. Most of the prisoners' families would not even visit because of the conditions. Prisoners were often bound at the ankle with shackles. They had to bend over and hold the shackle chain up to walk.

People were arrested and sent to jail not only for crimes but also for not being able to pay their debts. (A debt is money that has been borrowed from and owed to someone else.) John Wesley's father, Samuel, was often in debt and once was arrested at the door of his church because he could not immediately pay the debt. Samuel was kept in debtor's prison for three months. Susanna sent Samuel her wedding rings to sell to help pay for the debt, but Samuel refused to use the rings. Finally, Samuel's archbishop paid the debt so Samuel could be released from jail.

When John and Charles Wesley began the Holy Clubs, they went with the members to visit the jails. They told the prisoners the good news about Jesus. They helped debtors pay their debts whenever they could and cared for the sick prisoners.

◆ Shackles

Supplies: *construction paper, glue or stapler and staples*

- *Cut construction paper into 2-by-11-inch lengths. You will need four for each child.*

- *Give each child the four strips. Show the children how to glue or staple the strips together to make links.*

- *Have the jailer slip the links over each child's hands as if they are wearing handcuffs.*

◆ Visit the Prisoners

Supplies: *play money*

- *The other half of the Holy Club may go to the jail to visit the prisoners.*

- *Have the visitors say a prayer with the prisoners.*

- *The visitors should also bring their play money. Have the members give the jailer some of their money to pay the prisoner's debts. This will pay the debt in full and allow the prisoners to be released.*

The Wesley Home

Supplies: *Bible, desk and chair, rocker, kitchen table, quill pen (feather), candle, teapot and cups*

- *Continue to use the Wesley Home set up in Session 1.*

The Singing School

Supplies: *pp. 34-35*

- *Have the Holy Clubs move to The Wesley Home area and sit down.*
- *Teach the children three hymns written by Charles Wesley (pp. 34-35).*

Meet Charles Wesley

Supplies: *p. 52, costume for Charles Wesley*

- *Recruit a man to pretend to be Charles Wesley. Have the man wear a black ministerial robe.*
- *Give the man the script for Charles (page 52). Ask the man to use the script as a guideline and tell the story in his own words.*

Hear the Bible Story

Supplies: *p. 53, costume for Charles Wesley*

- *Give the man the script for the Bible story Charles is to tell (p 53).*
- *Have Charles hold the Bible as he tells the Bible story,"From Saul to Paul."*

The Forgotten Wesley

Supplies: *p. 54, costume for Charles Wesley*

- *Photocopy "The Forgotten Wesley" (p. 54) for the actors.*
- *Choose confident readers for narrator and Towne Crier. All the other characters are non-speaking roles.*
- *Have the actors present the play to the children.*

The Holy Clubs

Supplies: *p. 18, gingerbread cookies made earlier (pp. 45-46), hand-washing supplies, napkins, plastic spoons*

- *Have the children wash their hands and then return to their Holy Clubs.*
- *Sing "Be Present at Our Table, Lord."*
- *Let the children eat their gingerbread cookies.*

PRAY: Thank you, God, for people throughout history who taught others about your love. Amen.

Always check for allergies before handling or serving food to your children.

Money

Bible Cards

HOW	WONDERFUL	IS	THE
COMING	OF	MESSENGERS	WHO
BRING	GOOD	NEWS	ROMANS 10:15, Good News Translation

Charles Wesley

Do you remember me? I'm Charles Wesley. We met at the Singing School. I'm John's younger brother. Like John, I became a pastor in the Anglican Church. I started The Holy Clubs with John, and I went with him to Georgia to preach to Native Americans.

But like John, I did not have a good experience in the New World. Even though I was a pastor, I did not really believe in Jesus. Then one day I felt the Spirit of God inside of me. The Spirit changed my life and I believed!

I wrote many poems and hymns to help people learn the good news about Jesus. You may know at least one of them—"Hark! the Herald Angel Sings." John and I liked to write new words to songs people already knew and sang. Once several drunken sailors came into a Wesley meeting singing a popular song called "Nancy Dawson." I decided I liked the song's tune, but not the words the sailors were using. So I wrote new words to the popular tune. The sailors came back to the meeting the next day to find people singing a hymn to their song.

From Saul to Paul by LeeDell Stickler

I have told you that my life was changed when I realized how much God loves me. Let me tell you a Bible story about a man whose life was completely changed when he met Jesus.

"The followers of Jesus are just troublemakers. We must get rid of them. And I am just the man to do it," said Saul.

So Saul went from house to house to house in Jerusalem. He arrested every man, woman, and child who followed Jesus and had them put into prison.

But Saul didn't stop there. He knew there were many followers of Jesus who lived in other cities. "I must go to other cities and find these followers of Jesus. I will find them and have them arrested and thrown into prison—every man, every woman, every child."

Saul had heard that a group of followers were teaching and preaching in the city of Damascus. "I will go to Damascus. I will find these followers of Jesus. I will find them and have them arrested and thrown into prison—every man, every woman, every child."

So Saul gathered some soldiers to go with him as bodyguards. They set out on the road to Damascus. As the group drew near the city, suddenly a bright light shone all around Saul. Saul fell down to the ground.

From the light came a voice, "Saul, why are you doing this?"

"Who is this?" asked Saul. He was very afraid.

"I am Jesus, the one whose followers you are hurting. Get up now and go into the city. Wait and you will be told what you are to do."

The light faded away. Saul stumbled to his feet. "Help me!" he called out. "I can't see! Everything is dark!" Saul groped about, trying to feel his way. Saul's bodyguards had to lead him into the city. For three days Saul sat in darkness. He was too upset to eat or drink. He just waited, as Jesus had told him.

At the same time in another part of the city, there lived a man named Ananias. Ananias was a follower of Jesus. Jesus also appeared to him. "Get up and go to a house on Straight Street. There you will find a man named Saul. Lay your hands on him so that he might be able to see again."

"I have heard of this man," said Ananias. "He searches out followers of Jesus and has them arrested. Why would I want him to see again?"

"This is the man I have chosen to tell my story to the Gentiles," said Jesus.

And Ananias did as Jesus told him. He found the place where Saul was staying. "Brother Saul, the Lord Jesus has sent me so that you may regain your sight and be filled with the Holy Spirit."

As Ananias touched Saul, Saul's vision returned. Ananias baptized Saul. And from that day forward, Saul, the man who had hunted down the followers of Jesus, now preached the good news to every man, every woman, and every child who would listen. His life changed so much that he even began to be called by a new name. Now Saul was called Paul.

(Based on Acts 9:1-19.)

The Forgotten Wesley by Daphna Flegal

Characters:

Narrator   Charles Wesley

John Wesley   Peter Bohler

Bystander

Scene 1: A room at Christ Church, Oxford

Set: a wooden table with a chair, a candle on the table.

Narrator: Charles is sometimes referred to as "the forgotten Wesley" because his brother John is more famous. But Charles was important to the history of the Methodist Church.

Charles went to college to be a pastor. While he was at college, Charles kept having doubts about God. In order to feel closer to God, he started something called The Holy Club.

Charles: It's important that every member of the Holy Club does these things: Get up early; read the Bible; pray; and don't waste time.

John: I've made a list of rules for the club. It will give us a method for daily living.

Bystander: Ha! Those Holy Club members are a bunch of "methodists!"

Narrator: John, Charles, and the other club members didn't mind the name. They were too busy helping people who were poor, sick, and in prison.

Scene 2: A Trip to America

Set: a cardboard ship or items you'd find on a ship such as a steering wheel or fishnet or rope.

Narrator: Charles and John were asked by a man named General Olglethorpe to go to Georgia in the American colonies to preach to the Native Americans. It was not a successful trip.

John: We've been yelled at, shot at, and ignored. I'm glad to go back to England.

Narrator: It was on the ship ride home that Charles and John met a group of people called the Moravians.

Charles: Listen to them sing! Even during stormy weather at sea they sing their praises to God. I wish I had that kind of faith.

Narrator: After returning to England, Charles became friends with a Moravian named Peter Bohler. Peter and Charles talked about the doubts Charles still had about God.

Peter: Look deep into your heart, Charles. That's where you'll find your answers.

Scene 3: Conversion

Set: a wooden table with a chair, a candle on the table.

Narrator: That spring, Charles became ill. While he was in bed, he thought and prayed. Finally, on Pentecost Sunday he felt God's love for himself.

Charles: At last I've found peace for myself with God. I know I love Jesus!

Narrator: Three days later John had a similar experience when his heart was "strangely warmed." One year later, Charles wrote the hymn, "O For a Thousand Tongues to Sing," on the anniversary of his conversion.

Charles: Sing the first verse with me now:

> O for a thousand tongues to sing
>
> my great Redeemer's praise,
>
> the glories of my God and King,
>
> the triumphs of his grace!

Narrator: By the time he died, Charles had written over 5,000 hymns. Charles may be called the "forgotten Wesley," but because of Charles Wesley the people in the Methodist church became known as the "Singing Methodists."

The End

Session 4: Thomas Coke and Francis Asbury

Thomas Coke was sent to America after the War of Independence. He became the first American bishop. Thomas Coke ordained another man, Francis Asbury. Francis Asbury traveled 275,000 miles, mostly on horseback, to tell people the good news about Jesus.

Suggestions for Session 4

1. *Begin the Session in the Holy Clubs and play "Ride!" with the children.*
2. *Move to The Village Shoppes.*
3. *Choose all or some of the following shoppes:*
   The Village Inn: Taste Travel Foods
   The Candle Shoppe: Make Dipped Candles
   The Print Shoppe: Make Stamps
4. *Gather the children into a large group for the activities in The Ship.*
5. *Send the children back to their Holy Clubs to enjoy their snack and close the session.*

Volunteers Needed

- *Holy Club Leaders*
- *Shoppe Leaders: The Village Inn, The Candle Shoppe, The Print Shoppe*
- *Thomas Coke*
- *Francis Asbury*
- *Actors for "The Gospel Trailblazer"*

Holy Clubs

Meet With the Holy Clubs

Supplies: *p. 15, quilts, can with sand or gravel, dowel or stick*

- *Place quilts on the floor to designate each Holy Club.*
- *Photocopy the "Holy Club" sign (p. 15) for each club.*
- *Give the children their nametags.*

✦ Ride!

Supplies: *stick horses or brooms, chairs*

SAY: Circuit riders traveled on horseback from town to town, telling others the good news about Jesus. They traveled many, many miles. One circuit rider, Francis Asbury, traveled 275,000 miles.

- *Provide two or more stick horses or brooms.*
- *Place a chair at one end of the play area or have a person standing there. You will need as many chairs or people as you have stick horses or brooms.*
- *Have the children line up in relay teams at the opposite end of the play area from each chair or person.*
- *Give the first child in line the stick horse or broom.*
- *Shout, "Ride! Circuit rider, ride!"*
- *Have the children ride the stick horses or brooms around the chairs or people and back to their lines. Have the children give their horses or brooms to the next people in their lines. Continue until every child has a turn.*

Involve the children in the game as soon as they arrive.

✦ Tell About Circuit Riders

Supplies: *Bible, saddlebag made in Session 2*

SAY: The Methodist movement crossed the sea to the American colonies. Circuit riders traveled on horseback from town to town, telling others the good news about Jesus. Thomas Coke was sent to America after the War of Independence. He became the first American bishop. Thomas Coke ordained another man, Francis Asbury. Francis Asbury traveled 275,000 miles, mostly on horseback to tell people the good news about Jesus.

Francis Asbury set up the early American church into circuits. Each circuit was made up of several towns. A preacher traveled the circuit from town to town. It was often more than a month before the preacher returned to the same town. He traveled on his horse carrying everything he owned in his saddlebags. He often slept on the ground, even in rain and snow.

✦ Missions

- *Tell the children about any mission project your group is doing as part of Journey With J. W.*

✦ Learn the Bible Verse

Supplies: *Bible, Bible verse puzzle (p. 62), scissors, saddlebag*

"Look! I bring good news to you—wonderful, joyous news for all people."

Luke 2:10

- *Photocopy the Bible verse puzzle (p. 62). Cut the puzzle apart. Put the puzzle pieces in a saddlebag.*
- *Choose a child to read the Bible verse from the Bible.*
- *Pass the saddlebag to the children. Have each child take at least one piece of the puzzle out of the saddlebag. If you have less than twelve children in your group, some children will need to have more than one piece.*
- *Have the children work together to complete the puzzle. Say the Bible verse together.*

◆ Repeat Matthew 28:19

- *Repeat "Therefore, go and make disciples of all nations" (Matthew 28:19) with the children.*

The Village Shoppes

The Village Inn

Supplies: *baskets, wooden bowls, iron skillets, teapots, and churns*

- *Use the Village Inn set up from Session 1.*

◆ Taste Travel Foods

Supplies: *beef jerky, dried apples, English tea biscuits, napkins*

SAY: **The circuit riders traveled many thousands of miles to tell people the good news about Jesus. Francis Asbury traveled 275,000 miles, mostly on horseback. These circuit riders carried the food they were going to eat in their saddlebags.**

- *Let the children taste the foods.*

The Candle Shoppe

Supplies: *candles*

- *Display candles.*

SAY: **Candles were made at home by women and young children. One way to make candles was to use tallow, the fat from sheep or cattle. The tallow would be saved for months until there was enough to make the candles. The tallow was melted in iron kettles that hung over the fire in the fireplace. While the tallow was melting, the children tied candlewick string onto a thin stick. The women then took the wicks and dipped them into the hot tallow. Next they would hang the wicks on a hanging rack until the tallow became cool and hard. They dipped the candles over and over again until the candles were big enough to use.**

In colonial America, candles were often made from bayberries. Bayberry bushes have a waxy berry. The colonists would gather the berries and boil them in water.

Always check for allergies before handling or serving food to your children.

The wax floated to the top of the kettle as the berries boiled. The wax was skimmed off the top and allowed to harden. The wax was then melted to use for candle making. Bayberry candles smelled good as they burned. The colonists began making bayberry candles to ship to England.

Some women used candle molds to make candles. The molds allowed the women to make twenty or more candles at one time. The women set wicks in the mold and then poured in hot wax. This was much quicker than dipping candles.

◆ Dipped Candles

Supplies: *tall metal cans (coffee or juice cans), hot plate or stove, paraffin wax, crayons, candlewicking, sticks or unsharpened pencils, water, ice, sauce pans, newspapers, potholders*

- *Place a pan of water on a hot plate or stove. Set a tall metal can (coffee can, juice can) inside it. Turn the hot plate or stove on low heat.*
- *Put paraffin wax in the can to melt. Melt enough paraffin so that the can is about three-fourths full. Add crayons (with papers removed) to color the wax.*
- *Cut candlewicking into 18-inch lengths.*
- *Cover the work area with several layers of newspaper.*
- *Fill other cans with cold water. Set pans of ice in your work area. Place the cans of water in the pans of ice.*
- *Give each child a length of candlewicking and a stick or unsharpened pencil. Have the children tie one end of the wicking around the stick or pencil.*

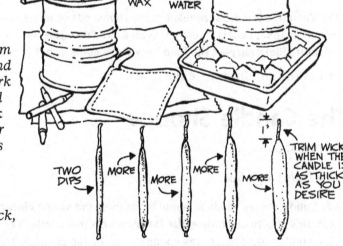

- *Use potholders to remove the can from the pan of water and place it in your work area. You will need to put the can back in the heated water as the wax hardens and needs to be reheated.*
- *Show the children how to hold the stick, dip the wick into the hot wax, and immediately dip the waxed string into the ice water. Let the children repeat this process until the candles are as thick as they want them to be.*
- *Trim the top of the wick to about one inch.*

The Print Shoppe

Supplies: *old books and newspapers*

- *Display old books and newspapers that you have available from your church or community library.*

SAY: The first printing press in Europe was invented by John Gutenberg in the 1400s. The press had type that could be moved, and it could print 300 to 500 sheets a day. This was amazing because up until Gutenberg's press, books were copied by hand. One of the first books Gutenberg printed on his press was the Bible.

The printing presses at the time of the Wesleys and the first circuit riders were very similar to the Gutenberg press. The type was made from small bits of lead and had a raised letter on one end. The type was arranged so that the letters that were used most were closest to the printer's hand. You had to be good at spelling to be a printer. The printer would take out the individual letters of type needed to spell each word. The letters were in a box called a composing stick. The printer tried to do this part as fast as he could. The faster the printer set the type, the sooner the newspaper or book could be printed. After setting the type, the printer rubbed ink over the type with a ball made of sheep's wool. The composing stick was placed in the press underneath paper. The printer then used his hands and feet to operate the printing machine. When a printer published books, he would stitch the pages together with needle and thread. Early print shops made newspapers, books, and magazines.

✦ Make Stamps

Supplies: *p. 42; wood blocks; fine sandpaper; thin foam sheets, foam innersoles for shoes, or recycled plastic foam trays; wide rubber bands; pencils; scissors; nonpermanent stamp pads; glue; lunch-size paper bags*

- *Cut wood into blocks about 1½-by-2-by-¾ inches.*
- *Cut thin foam sheets, foam innersoles for shoes, or recycled plastic foam trays into rectangles about 1-by-1½ inches.*
- *Or cut wide rubber bands into strips.*
- *Give each child a wood block and piece of sandpaper. Show the children how to sand the edges of the wood blocks to make them smooth.*

Foam Stamps:

- *Show the children the symbols poster (p. 42). Talk about each symbol.*
- *Give each child a foam rectangle and a pencil. (You may need light colored pencils for the innersoles.) Let the children draw a symbol on the foam. Have the children cut out the foam symbols.*
- *Have the children glue their foam symbols onto their wood blocks. Let the glue dry.*

Rubber Band Stamps:

- *Give each child several rubber band strips.*
- *Let the children cut the strips into short pieces.*

- *Have the children glue the rubber band pieces into patterns on their wood blocks. Let the glue dry.*

✦ *Stamp It*

- *Show the children how to press the stamps onto the nonpermanent ink pads and then onto paper.*

- *Encourage the children to use their stamps to make stationary, cards, or gift tags. The children might make cards for persons in the hospital or with limited ability to leave home. Ask your church secretary for a list of names, and mail the cards yourself or give the cards to your pastor to distribute.*

- *Or let the children use their stamps to decorate lunch-size paper bags. Provide wrapped candy or other small gifts (sample-size hand cream, pocket tissues, boxes of raisins, note pads, and so forth) for the children to put into the bags. Give the bags to an older adult group in your church.*

- *Remind the children that the early Methodists cared about others.*

The Ship

Supplies: *Bible, large appliance box, cardboard, duct tape*

- *Change the Wesley home scene to a clipper ship.*

- *Make a ship out of a large appliance box. If you have support posts in your room, use a post to be the ship's mast. Cut the box to fit around the post. Or make a mast out of cardboard. Cut one side from a large appliance box. Roll the side into a tube shape. Split one end of the tube and fold the ends out to make supports for the tube. Tape the tube inside the box ship.*

The Singing School

Supplies: *pp. 34-35*

- *Have the Holy Clubs move to The Ship area and sit down.*

- *Teach the children three hymns written by Charles Wesley (pp. 34-35).*

Meet Thomas Coke

Supplies: *p. 63, costume for Thomas Coke*

- *Recruit a man to pretend to be Thomas Coke. Have the man dress in a costume including a black ministerial robe and a white collar.*
- *Give the man the script for Thomas Coke (page 63). Ask the man to use the script as a guideline and tell the story in his own words.*

Hear the Bible Story

Supplies: *p. 64, costume for Thomas Coke*

- *Give the man the script for the Bible story Thomas is to tell (p. 64).*
- *Have Thomas hold the Bible as he tells the Bible story, "The Fishermen."*

The Gospel Trailblazer

Supplies: *pp. 65-66, bell, rocking chair, baby doll, stick horse, deck of cards, horseshoe or horseshoe made from cardboard, wig*

- *Photocopy "The Gospel Trailblazer" (p. 65-66) for the actors.*
- *Choose confident readers for narrator and Towne Crier. All the other characters are non-speaking roles.*

The Holy Clubs

Supplies: *p. 18, travel foods (p. 57), hand-washing supplies, napkins*

- *Have the children wash their hands and then return to their Holy Clubs.*
- *Sing "Be Present at Our Table, Lord."*
- *Let the children eat more of the travel foods.*

PRAY: **Thank you, God, for people throughout history who taught others about your love. Amen.**

Always check for allergies before handling or serving food to your children.

Look!
I bring good news to you— wonderful, joyous news for all people.

Luke 2:10

Thomas Coke

Thomas Coke

My name is Thomas Coke. I met John Wesley when John was seventy-three years old. That meeting completely changed my life. When I met John, I was a pastor in the Church of England. John wanted me to become a Methodist and be his assistant. I accepted the job. John made me the General Superintendent for America. I sailed to the United States and helped spread the Methodist movement there. One of the first things I did was ordain Francis Asbury as a general superintendent. Later, we were called bishops. I helped set up the rules of the new church in America. The new church was called the Methodist Episcopal Church.

But my travels did not end in America. I sailed to Nova Scotia, the West Indies, and other parts of the world. I wanted to start Methodist missions all over the world

The Fishermen by LeeDell Stickler

The lake shore was very busy on this fine morning. People from the village had come to purchase fish for their daily meals. But there were few fish to be had.

Many fishermen had given up for the day. They pulled their boats onto the sand and were washing their nets. The boats stood empty. Maybe tomorrow would be a better day.

As Simon washed his net, a man walked up to him. "May I use your boat? If I teach from your boat, then everyone can hear." Simon, who was also called Peter, agreed, and Jesus climbed into the boat. Peter pushed the boat out into the water, a little way from the shore.

Jesus sat down and began teaching the people. When he had finished speaking, he said to Simon, "Put out into the deep water. Let down your nets for a catch."

Peter just shook his head, "Teacher, we have worked all night long and didn't catch a thing. I don't think it will do any good. But I will do as you say."

Peter lowered the nets over the side of the boat. Soon there were so many fish in the net that the small boat almost sank.

"Help us," Peter called out to the other fishermen on the shore. Soon the other boats were filled with so many fish that they were about to sink as well.

Peter looked at the man who was sitting in his boat. He was afraid.

"Don't be afraid, Peter," said Jesus. "From now on you will be catching people."

When Peter had brought the boats into shore, he and his brother, Andrew, and James and John left their nets, their boats, and their families and followed Jesus.

That's quite a story, isn't it? You know sometimes when the days seem long and hard, I think about that Bible story. It always gives me new strength because I know I am doing God's work; I am catching people for Jesus.

(Based on Luke 5:1-11.)

The Gospel Trailblazer by LeeDell Stickler

Characters:

Towne Crier	Narrator
Elizabeth Asbury (Francis' mother)	
Francis Asbury, boy	Francis as young man
Francis as man	Older Francis
Thomas Coke	Men playing cards
Soldiers	Two Helpers

Props: *bell, one rocking chair, baby doll, stick horse, deck of cards, horseshoe or horseshoe made from cardboard, and a wig (for older Francis). Optional: costumes and a tricorn hat (for the towne crier)*

Drama Notes: *This drama is styled after the French tableaux vivant. The actors create frozen pictures that tell the story of the scene. Usually this is done without words. This drama has been adapted to have a narrator in order for the children to hear the historical information. Select children to be the characters in the tableau. Explain the scenes they are creating and the suggested poses. Give the children a few minutes to practice their poses. Then begin the tableau. Have the children stay in the audience until it is their turn to be on stage.*

Narrator: Today our play is a tableau vivant or living picture. That means the actors freeze in a picture to tell the story. Each scene has its own frozen frame. When the scene changes, people in the audience are to close their eyes. I will say curtain down when you are to close your eyes. When the towne crier says curtain up, you are to open your eyes. Let's begin. Curtain down.

(Elizabeth Asbury: Enters stage. Sits in rocking chair and holds baby doll. Elizabeth freezes.)

Towne Crier: Curtain up. 1745 and all is well for Elizabeth Asbury. *(Rings bell.)*

Narrator: Elizabeth Asbury had a strange dream. She dreamed that God spoke to her and told her that her baby was going to be a great religious leader some day. Her baby was named Francis Asbury. Curtain down.

(Elizabeth Asbury exits stage.)

(Francis Asbury—boy: Enters stage. Kneels and folds hands in prayer. Freezes.)

Towne Crier: Curtain up. 1751 and all is well for for the boy, Francis. *(Rings bell.)*

Narrator: The children at school called Francis the "Methodist Parson." They thought he was too serious, but all he wanted to do was please God. He promised never to lie, swear, fight, or be as lighthearted as his friends. He wanted to do good and be good. Curtain down.

(The boy Francis exits stage.)

(Francis as young man: Enters stage. Pretends to pound on a horseshoe. Freezes.)

Towne Crier: Curtain up. 1758 and all is well for the young man, Francis Asbury. *(Rings bell.)*

Narrator: Francis was apprenticed to a family to be a blacksmith. Being a blacksmith gave him lots of time to think about God. One day a pious man visited the neighborhood. Francis's mother invited him to the house. After listening to him, Francis felt his life begin to change. Francis asked his mother where he could find these "Methodists." Curtain down.

(Francis as young man exits.)

(Francis as man: Enters stage. Stands with arms raised as if preaching. Freezes.)

Towne Crier: Curtain up. 1767 and all is well for the man, Francis Asbury. *(Rings bell.)*

Narrator: Francis was quite taken by the preaching of these people called Methodists. He had heard John Wesley preach. John Wesley appointed him to be a traveling preacher. He preached anywhere he could draw a crowd—in the fields, in barns, in homes, on street corners, in the market place, or even in the mines. Curtain down.

(Francis Asbury: Changes position. He sits on the floor, holding his stomach and mouth as if seasick. Freezes.)

Towne Crier: Curtain up. 1771 and all is not well for Francis Asbury. *(Rings bell.)*

Narrator: John Wesley asked Francis to go to America. Francis agreed to go. Francis had never been so sick in his whole life as he was during the journey. The ship turned up and down and from side to side. But he did not waste an opportunity to tell people about God. Not many people on board were interested. But Francis promised to live for God and bring others to do so as well. Curtain down.

(Francis Asbury: Changes position. He rides a stick horse. Freezes.)

Towne Crier: Curtain up. 1771 and all is well for Francis Asbury. *(Rings bell.)*

Narrator: Most of the people of this New World lived in the country. If the Word of God was going to get to them, Francis knew he would have to take it to them on horseback. Curtain down.

(Men playing cards and Francis Asbury: Men enter and sit at table or floor. Hold cards as if playing a game. Francis stands to one side watching men. Looks disapproving. Freeze.)

Towne Crier: Curtain up. 1774 and all is not well for Francis Asbury. *(Rings bell.)*

Narrator: Sometimes Francis got discouraged. It seemed that Americans were unwilling to give up their dancing, card playing, and laziness. Francis thought about barring these "half-hearted Methodists" from the meetings. People did not take this so well. There were rumors about riding Francis out of town. Curtain down.

(Men playing cards exit.)

(Soldiers and Francis Asbury: Soldiers enter stage. Pretend to be in battle. Francis turns back to soldiers. Freeze.)

Towne Crier: Curtain up. 1776 and all is not well for Francis Asbury. *(Rings bell.)*

Narrator: The colonies were at war! The fighting became heavier and heavier. Even though Francis was a preacher, many people were suspicious of him because he was English. Some colonies wanted him to take a loyalty oath. But Francis would only take an oath to God. He would not carry a gun and fight for either side. The other preachers had deserted him. He was then the only traveling English preacher in America. Curtain down.

(Soldiers exit stage.)

(Thomas Coke and Francis Asbury: Thomas Coke enters stage. Francis kneels in front of Thomas Coke. Thomas Coke puts his hands on Francis' head. Freeze.)

Towne Crier: Curtain up. 1784 and all is well for Francis Asbury. *(Rings bell.)*

Narrator: The war was over. John Wesley sent Thomas Coke to America to ordain ministers. He consecrated Francis Asbury as a bishop. For seventeen years he had been traveling about the country preaching the gospel. Now Francis Asbury and Thomas Coke were in charge of Methodism in America. Curtain down.

(Thomas Coke and Francis Asbury exit stage.)

(Older Francis and Two Helpers: Older Francis enters stage wearing wig. Two helpers help him walk. Freeze.)

Towne Crier: Curtain up. 1815 and all is well for Francis Asbury. *(Rings bell.)*

Narrator: Bishop Asbury kept traveling even when he was an older man. He was in such poor health that he had to be carried about like a little child. He saw the church grow from 600 or so members when he first arrived in America to 214,000 members. Although the Methodist Church had many great and good teachers, she had but one father under God, and that was Francis Asbury. Curtain down.

The End

Session 5: Richard Allen

Richard Allen was born a slave but was able to buy his freedom. He worked as a woodcutter, a bricklayer, and a salt wagon driver. Then he became a businessman.

Richard was also a Christian. He heard Methodist preachers tell the good news about Jesus, and he began to preach and organize prayer meetings.

Suggestions for Session 5

1. *Begin the Session in the Holy Clubs and play "Hoops" with the children.*
2. *Move to The Village Shoppes.*
3. *Choose all or some of the following shoppes:*
   The Village Inn: Make Johnnycake
   The Farm: Plant Corn, Make Cornhusk Dolls
   The Quilting Bee: Make a Quilt
4. *Gather the children into a large group for the activities in*
   A Colonial Church.
5. *Send the children back to their Holy Clubs to enjoy their snacks*
   and close the session.

Volunteers Needed

- *Holy Club Leaders*
- *Shoppe Leaders: The Village Inn, The Farm, The Quilting Bee*
- *Richard Allen*
- *Actors for "In the Land of the Wyandots"*

Holy Clubs

Meet With the Holy Clubs

Supplies: *p. 15, quilts, can with sand or gravel, dowel or stick*

- *Place quilts on the floor to designate each Holy Club.*
- *Photocopy the "Holy Club" sign (p. 15) for each club.*
- *Give the children their nametags.*

✦ Hoops

Supplies: *wooden or metal hoops or hula hoops; sticks, dowels, or paint stirrers*

SAY: Rolling hoops was a favorite game for children. Hoops were made of metal or wood from old barrels. Children used sticks to tap the hoops and keep them rolling on their edges.

- *If wooden or metal hoops are available, let the children enjoy rolling these more authentic hoops.*
- *Or purchase hula hoops, and let the children try to keep the hoops rolling on their edges. Sticks, dowels, or paint stirrers may be used to guide the hoops. Paint stirrers are usually free at paint or home improvement stores.*
- *Make hoop rolling into a relay game. Place a chair or have a person stand at one end of the play area. You will need as many chairs or people as you have sticks and hoops.*
- *Have the children line up in relay teams at the opposite end of the play area from each chair or person.*
- *Give the first child in line the hoop and stick.*
- *Shout, "Ready, set, roll!"*

Involve the children in the game as soon as they arrive.

✦ Tell About Camp Meetings

SAY: Camp meetings were times for many people to come together for worship and fellowship. Camp meetings usually were held once or twice a year. Sometimes as many as one thousand people would come to the meetings. Families would set up camp and stay for five to ten days. People would meet together for hours at a time. The best preacher in the area would preach, and people would sing hymns. Hundreds of people would become Christians at the camp meetings.

If you are closing your event with a camp meeting, explain to the children what will happen. Make sure the children know if their parents are invited.

✦ Missions

- *Tell the children about any mission project your group is doing as part of Journey With J. W.*

✦ Learn the Bible Verse

Supplies: *Bible, p. 74, scissors, string or clothesline, clothespins*

"You will be his witness to everyone
concerning what you have seen and heard."
Acts 22:15

- *Photocopy the Bible verse cards (p. 74). Cut the cards apart.*
- *Choose a child to read the Bible verse from the Bible.*

- *Have two children hold a string or clothesline between them. Clothespin the cards to the line in order of the Bible verse. Say the Bible verse together.*
- *Take away one of the word cards. Have the children say the Bible verse, filling in the missing word.*
- *Continue until the children say the Bible verse without any word cards.*

✦ Repeat Matthew 28:19

- *Repeat "Therefore, go and make disciples of all nations" (Matthew 28:19) with the children.*

The Village Shoppes

The Village Inn

Supplies: *baskets, wooden bowls, iron skillets, teapots, and churns*

- *Use the Village Inn set up from Session 1.*

✦ Johnny Cake

Supplies: *Johnny Cake ingredients, mixing bowl, mixing spoon, measuring cups and spoons, electric skillet*

- *Melt ⅔ cup shortening or oil in an electric skillet.*
- *Have the children wash their hands.*
- *Use the recipe below with the children. Have the children take turns as they work together.*

Johnnycake

1 cup cornmeal	pinch of salt
3 tsp. baking powder	¾ cup hot water
2 eggs	

- *Have the children measure the cornmeal, salt, and baking powder and pour into large bowl. Mix together.*
- *Stir in water to make a paste.*
- *Add eggs and beat well.*
- *Adults only: Use a teaspoon to drop batter into oil. Cook until golden brown.*
- *Makes about 24–30 small cakes.*
- *Let the cakes cool until time for the Holy Clubs at the end of the session.*

Always have adult supervision when using electric skillets around children. Be sure to plug in skillets in a place where children cannot trip over the cords.

Always check for allergies before handling or serving food to your children.

The Farm

Supplies: *artificial flowers, seed packages, and garden tools*

- *Display artificial flowers, seed packages, and garden tools.*

SAY: Farming was important in both England and the American colonies during the time of John Wesley. Wealthy people had large farms with grain, fruit and vegetables, and animals such as cows, sheep, pigs, and chickens.

Gardens were usually split into two sections. One side was planted with herbs and vegetables. The other side was planted with flowers. In the American colonies tomatoes were planted in the flower gardens. Colonists thought tomatoes were pretty, but they would never eat them. Most people thought tomatoes were poisonous.

In the American colonies, people often helped each other with the work that needed to be done on the farm. People would get together in working bees to do things like husk corn or prepare apples for making apple sauce or apple cider. The working bees usually ended in a party.

✦ Plant Corn

Supplies: *corn on the cob or picture of corn, pie pans, spoons, potting soil, popcorn kernels, water, watering can, paper or plastic table covering.*

SAY: Corn was a common food in the American colonies. Corn was ground into cornmeal. The meal was then mixed with water or milk, salt, and lard to make cornbread. Cornbread had different names in different places. Sometimes it was called cornpone, hoecake, or johnnycake.

- *Provide supplies for planting corn.*
- *Cover the work space with paper or plastic.*
- *Have an ear of corn (or a picture of corn) and cornmeal to show the children.*
- *Let the children make a miniature cornfield.*
- *Give each child a pie pan. Let the children spoon potting soil into the bottom of their pie pans.*
- *Let the children plant popcorn kernels in the soil. Tell the children that on a farm, corn is usually planted in rows.*
- *Let the children lightly water the corn.*

✦ Cornhusk Dolls

Supplies: *p. 75, cornhusks (12 per doll), string or yarn cut into six-inch lengths, scissors, optional: felt-tip pens*

SAY: The settlers who came to the American colonies were taught to make cornhusk dolls by the Native Americans. Dolls were also made out of corncobs, apples, and even cucumbers.

JOURNEY with J.W.

This activity is a good opportunity for children to help each other. One child can hold the cornhusks while the other child ties the string.

- *Purchase cornhusks from a craft store or grocery store (look in the Mexican food section). You will need twelve husks per doll.*
- *Cut string or yarn into 6-inch lengths.*
- *Photocopy the directions for making cornhusk dolls (p. 75).*
- *Give each child twelve corn husks and seven pieces of string or yarn.*
- *Show the children how to gather the twelve corn husks together. Help the children use a piece of string or yarn to tie the corn husks tightly together at one end. (See figure 1, p. 75.)*
- *Have the children use another piece of string or yarn to tie the corn husks two- to three-inches down from the first knot. This will make the head. (See figure 2.)*
- *Have the children gather three cornhusks on one side to make an arm. Help the children measure about halfway down the husks. Use a piece of string or yarn to tie the three husks together. Cut the extra arm husks off, leaving only a small amount to be the hands. Repeat on the other side. (See figure 3.)*
- *Have the children measure the remaining cornhusks halfway between the neck and the ends of the husks. Help the children use a piece of string or yarn to tie around the husks to make the waist. (See figure 4.)*
- *To make a girl doll, leave the remaining cornhusks untied to make a skirt. (See figure 4.)*
- *To make a boy doll, show the children how to make legs. Have the children gather three cornhusks on one side. Use a piece of string or yarn to tie the three husks together near the ends of the cornhusks. Repeat on the other side. (See figure 5.)*
- *Optional: Use felt-tip pens to make faces.*

The Quilting Bee

Supplies: *quilts*

- *Display quilts.*

SAY: Sometimes women worked together to make quilts at quilting bees. When the quilts were finished, the women's families came for supper, dancing, and games.

Quilts were made from scraps of cloth or from cutting up old clothing. The scraps of cloth were sewn into larger patches. The patches were then sewn together to make the whole quilt. The patches made up the repeating design of the quilt. The designs had names like "The Wedding Ring" or "The Carpenter's Square."

After the top of the quilt was pieced together, the top was laid on layers of wool and cotton wadding and a bottom lining. At a quilt bee the quilt was stretched over a big frame. Women would sit around the frame and stitch all the layers together. Children often sat under the quilt to pass the needles back to the top layer or pick up dropped needles.

✦ Make a Quilt

Supplies: *muslin, white paper, fabric crayons, scissors, iron, newspaper*

- Cut muslin into 12-inch squares.
- Cut white paper into 12-inch squares.
- Give each child a square of white paper. Let the children color a picture or design on the paper using the fabric crayons. Remind the children that their picture will transfer onto the fabric backwards.
- Have an adult set up and use an iron. Turn the iron onto the cotton setting. Have several layers of newspaper covered with white paper for an ironing pad.
- When each child finishes his or her picture, have the child bring the picture to the adult operating the iron. Lay the muslin square on the ironing pad. Place the colored pictured face down on the muslin. Press the iron over the entire design until the image shows through the back of the paper. Carefully remove the colored picture from the fabric.

✦ Finishing the Quilt

Supplies: *posterboard, scissors, quilt squares made earlier, glue, paper punch, yarn*

- Cut colorful posterboard into 14-inch squares.
- Let the children choose pieces of colored posterboard to go with their muslin squares. Have the children glue their muslin squares in the center of the posterboard squares.
- Use a paper punch to make two holes in the top of the posterboard. Thread a length of yarn through the holes and tie the ends together to make a hanger.
- Use the muslin square as a quilt wall hanging.

A Colonial Church

Supplies: *Bible, wooden benches or chairs, altar, lectern or podium, candles*

- Change the ship scene to the inside of a colonial church.
- Set up wooden benches or chairs, an altar, and a lectern or podium
- Add a Bible and candles.

The Singing School

Supplies: *pp. 34-35*

- Have the Holy Clubs move to A Colonial Church area and sit down.
- Teach the children three hymns written by Charles Wesley (pp. 34-35).

Meet Richard Allen

Supplies: *p. 76, costume for Richard Allen*

- *Recruit a man to pretend to be Richard Allen. Have the man dress in a costume including knee breeches, shirt, and a vest. If possible, have a tricorn hat.*
- *Give the man the script for Richard Allen (page 76). Ask the man to use the script as a guideline and tell the story in his own words.*

Hear the Bible Story

Supplies: *p. 77, costume for Richard Allen*

- *Give the man the script for the Bible story Richard is to tell (p. 77).*
- *Have Richard hold the Bible as he tells the Bible story, "Wind and Flame."*

In the Land of the Wyandots

Supplies: *pp. 78-79, old sheet or bulletin board paper, paint.*

- *Photocopy "In the Land of the Wyandots" (pp. 78-79) for the actors.*
- *Choose confident readers for Wyandot Woman, Wyandot Child, Wyandot Warrior, Jonathan Pointer, Chief Adam Brown, Jonathan Pointer, John Stewart*
- *Have the actors present the drama to the children.*
- *Let nonreaders be the audience and respond to the sidekick's directions.*

The Holy Clubs

Supplies: *p. 18, johnny cakes made earlier (p. 63), butter, hand-washing supplies, napkins, plastic spoons*

- *Have the children wash their hands and then return to their Holy Clubs.*
- *Sing "Be Present at Our Table, Lord."*
- *Let the children eat the johnny cakes. Let the children add butter if desired.*

PRAY: Thank you, God, for people throughout history who taught others about your love. Amen.

Always check for allergies before handling or serving food to your children.

HIS	CONCERNING	SEEN	
BE	EVERYONE	HAVE	Acts 22:15
WILL	TO	YOU	HEARD
YOU	WITNESS	WHAT	AND

Cornhusk Dolls

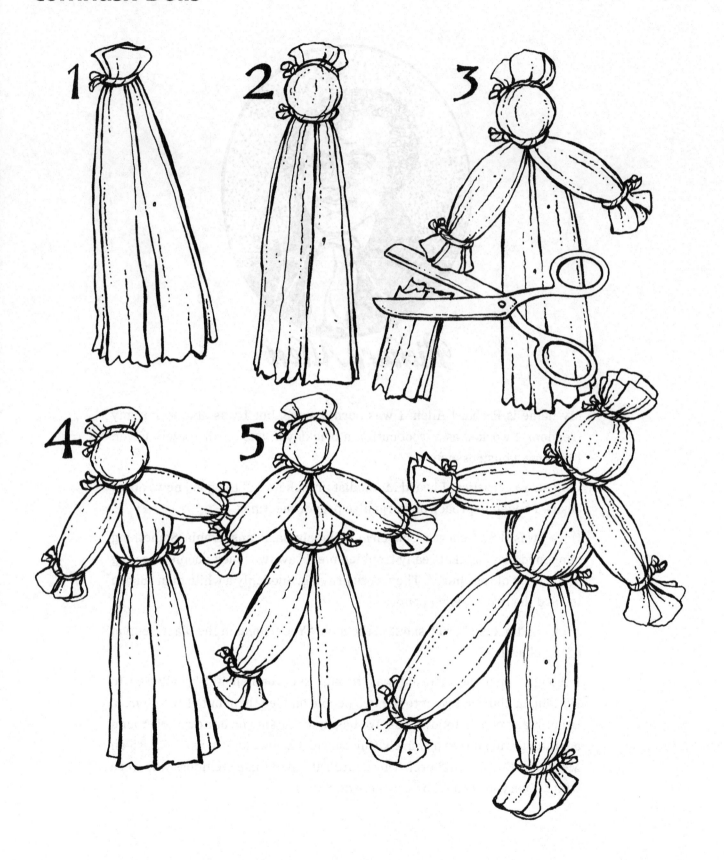

Richard Allen

My name is Richard Allen. I was born a slave, but I was able to buy my freedom. I worked as a woodcutter, a bricklayer, and a salt wagon driver. I became a businessman.

I am also a Christian. I heard Methodist preachers tell the good news about Jesus. I began to preach and organize prayer meetings.

Once I was at St. George's Church in Philadelphia, Pennsylvania. Something happened that day that really troubled me. I saw two black people kneeling at the front of the church. They were praying. Suddenly a white man rushed toward the two kneeling people.

"You don't belong here!" shouted the man. "You belong in the black section of the church."

I thought what the man did was wrong. Everyone should be allowed to worship in church. I went to the two people and led them out of the church. Other black people followed us. We began to worship on our own. We found a building and started a church. Our church became known as The African Methodist Episcopal Church. Our church also had some members who were white. Everyone should be welcome at church.

Wind and Flame by LeeDell Stickler

There was an unexpected wind
And dancing tongues of flame.
The Holy Spirit filled each one,
And they glorified God's name.

Many days had passed since Jesus had been crucified and raised from the dead. Jesus had told his disciples to go into all the world and tell everyone about him. Jesus had also promised that God would send a helper—a helper that would fill them with great power. With this power, they would be able to spread the good news of Jesus to all the earth.

What would this helper be like? How would they know when the helper came? What would it feel like to be filled with great power? No one knew, and so they waited.

For Jesus' followers, Pentecost was a celebration of the harvest. People gathered together to thank God and to make an offering of food at the Temple. After the offering, all of Jesus' followers were gathered in a room to eat together. Suddenly, there came a sound…the sound of a loud wind. What was going on? Everyone looked about. Then tongues of flame rested on the head of each person present that day. Everyone began to speak. But they spoke in languages different from their own. But everyone understood.

The noise in the room was so loud that people on the street heard the great commotion. "What is happening here?" they asked. "Why are these people speaking in different languages? What does it all mean?"

Peter raised his voice above the crowd and said, "All of you, let this be known. These people have been filled with the Holy Spirit. What has happened here is what the prophet said would happen. 'I will pour my spirit out onto all persons. And they will prophesy. And all who call on the name of the Lord will be saved.'"

When Peter had everyone's attention, he began to preach, "Let me tell you about a man called Jesus of Nazareth. He came to us and did wonderful things in the name of God. But he was not welcomed by his people. This man was the one you turned over to be crucified. Death did not stop him. God raised him from the dead because Jesus was truly God's Son."

Peter spoke on and on, telling the people more about Jesus. When he had finished, the people were touched to the heart. "What shall we do?" they asked Peter.

"Repent and be baptized in the name of Jesus Christ," Peter said. "You will be filled with the Holy Spirit as well. This is God's promise to you and to your children." And that day three thousand persons became followers of Jesus.

When people say to me, "You can't come here because you are black," I feel hurt and angry. Then I remember that Jesus knows how it feels to be laughed at and rejected. I remember that no matter what other people may say or do, there is one who always loves me. I am a follower of Jesus. Jesus loves me.

There was an unexpected wind
And dancing tongues of flame.
The Holy Spirit filled each one,
And they glorified God's name.

(Based on Acts 2.)

In the Land of the Wyandots by LeeDell Stickler

Characters:

Wyandot Woman   Wyandot Child

Wyandot Warrior

Jonathan Pointer (African American boy)

Chief Adam Brown
(Caucasian captive who rose to become chief)

Jonathan Pointer
(adult, respected member of Wyandot tribe)

John Stewart (African American missionary)

Set: Make a backdrop from an old sheet or bulletin board paper. Paint a woods scene on the back drop.

Scene I: Wyandot village. A hunting party is returning.

Off stage: Sound of excited shouts and whoops.

Wyandot Woman: I hear the hunting party returning. From the noise it sounds as though they have brought back a prisoner to the village.

Wyandot Child: Look! Do you see what I see? It's just a little boy. Look how scared he is! He's so skinny! And his skin. It is so dark, darker than ours.

Wyandot Woman: He does not know how lucky he is. Our warriors rarely take prisoners. They have brought him back here to become a part of our village.

Narrator: The Wyandot nation was a people who were proud and independent. Anyone who was brought as a captive to one of their villages was never mistreated. In fact, Jonathan, who had been a slave when he was captured, was treated with more kindness as a captive than he had experienced as a slave. Jonathan received food and warmth from the warrior who had captured Jonathan. But Jonathan did not always make life easy for them.

Wyandot Warrior: Jonathan is a smart boy. He has already learned our language. But he is intentionally disobedient. He is nothing but trouble.

Chief Adam Brown: Do not harm the boy. I will give you supplies, and you will give me the boy.

Narrator: And so the trade was made. Jonathan was happy. The Wyandot warrior was glad to be rid of such a troublesome boy. And Chief Adam Brown was happy. Chief Brown had been captured by the Delaware Indians when he was just a boy, so he had an idea of how Jonathan felt. But even though Jonathan's life was happier, he was still a troublemaker.

Chief Adam Brown: Jonathan, we have traders in our village tonight. They will buy the furs from our winter hunt and in return give us cooking pots and hunting knives. You must watch the horses for them so they don't stray.

Jonathan (boy): I will do that.

Narrator: Many times during the night, a horse would stray from the camp. Each time Jonathan went in search of the horse. The traders always rewarded him with a few coins. Soon the traders became suspicious at how many horses were straying. They discovered that Jonathan was letting the horses loose so they would pay him to get the horses back.

Chief Adam Brown: You deceitful boy! When the traders have left the village, you will be punished for what you have done.

Jonathan (boy): I don't want to be punished. I'll run away.

Narrator: And so Jonathan left the village that night and took refuge in another Wyandot village. But after awhile, Jonathan had to find another home. Jonathan went to live in the home of Chief Tarhe, an honored Wyandot chief.

Scene II: Jonathan Pointer's hut

Jonathan (man): (hears tapping outside the door) Who is it?

John Stewart: My name is John Stewart. I want to preach the Christian message to the Wyandots. I need an interpreter. Would you introduce me to the tribes? Would you interpret my words to them?

Jonathan (man): Why do you want to preach to the Wyandots?

John Stewart: I was born in Virginia. My parents moved to Tennessee and left me behind. Because of this, I got into all kinds of trouble. One day I passed a Methodist prayer meeting. I stepped inside and my life was changed. One night when I was praying, I heard a voice that said, "you must declare my council faithfully." Before I knew it, I was on my feet preaching to the trees and the grass as though they were people. I knew I needed to follow God. I headed northwest on foot. Each time I stopped, I felt God was urging me on. Then I knew God was telling me to come here.

Jonathan (man): It is a foolish idea for you to think that you, a man of color, can turn the Wyandots from their religion to a new one. Why should they listen to you?

John Stewart: By myself I can do nothing, but God will help me.

Narrator: The next day Jonathan had planned to attend a special feast and dance.

John Stewart: Please take me along. I will not be a burden to you. Just introduce me to the chiefs as a friend of their souls.

Jonathan: *(aloud but to himself)* Humph! This preacher is certain to spoil the fun of the celebration.

Narrator: That night John Stewart gave a short talk and sang a hymn or two. He invited the Wyandots to come back the next day. But the next day only one old woman showed up. John Stewart didn't get discouraged. He preached through Jonathan Pointer as though an entire congregation was in front of him. On the second day only two persons showed up. On the following day, there were a few more.

Jonathan (man): John, I did not think you would succeed. But every day more people come to hear you preach. There will soon be too many to worship in my small hut. Perhaps the Wyandots will let us use the council house.

Narrator: The number of Christians among the Wyandots grew slowly. But soon John learned that Jonathan was sometimes leaving out some of John's words. Sometimes Jonathan would add, "I don't know if this is true or not. These are his words, not mine."

John: *(to Jonathan)* Why are you leaving out some of my words?

Jonathan (man): I do not like you, and I do not like this new religion. When I agreed to be your interpreter, I did not say I would believe all you said. I just wanted to know what you were doing.

John: When you change my words or leave parts out, you are changing the meaning of the message.

Narrator: John Stewart spent much time with Jonathan. He told him what it meant to be a Christian. The two men prayed together. Finally, Jonathan accepted Christ. After his conversion, Jonathan took joy in his work, and the two became close and loving friends. Since this early time, the mission of the church has reached out to almost every country and tribe in the world. John Stewart was called by God as a Methodist missionary. And Jonathan Pointer, an unbelieving interpreter, soon became a dedicated follower.

The End

John Wesley's Sayings

Do all the good you can,

By all the ways you can,

In all the places you can,

At all the times you can,

To all the people you can,

As long as ever you can.

The world is my parish.

In the evening I went very unwillingly to a society in Aldersgate Street, where one was reading Luther's preface to the Epistle to the Romans. About a quarter before nine, while he was describing the change which God works in the heart through faith in Christ, I felt my heart strangely warmed. I felt I did trust in Christ, Christ alone for salvation; and an assurance was given me that he had taken away my sins, even mine, and saved me from the law of sin and death.

John Wesley's Journal

I stood near the east end of the church, upon my father's tombstone, and cried, "The kingdom of heaven is not meat and drink; but righteousness, and peace, and joy in the Holy Ghost."

John Wesley's Journal

At eight in the evening I stood again on my father's tomb (as I did every evening this week), and cried aloud to the earnestly attentive congregation, "By grace are ye saved through faith."

John Wesley's Journal

1 John 4:19. We love him, because he first loved us—This is the sum of all religion, the genuine model of Christianity. None can say more; why should any say less, or less intelligibly?

Explanatory Notes Upon the New Testament from John Wesley's Journal

Gain all you can.

Save all you can.

Give all you can.

Camp Meeting

Close your *Journey With J.W.* event with a camp meeting. Camp meetings were times for many people to come together for worship and fellowship. Camp meetings were usually held once or twice a year. Sometimes as many as one thousand people would come to the meetings. Families would set up camp and stay for five to ten days. People would meet together for hours at a time. The best preacher in the area would preach, and people would sing hymns. Hundreds of people would become Christians at the camp meetings.

Invite parents and friends to join in the fun. Plan for an open house with food and fellowship. Close with a time of worship. Use the suggestions below to plan the camp meeting.

Suggestions for Camp Meeting

1. *Begin the Camp Meeting at The Village Inn to make apple muffins. This will allow time for the apple muffins to bake.*
2. *Move to The Village Square to play games.*
3. *Gather everyone into a large group for Worship.*
4. *Present the participation pageant, "A Quick Ride Through History."*
5. *Eat the apple muffins.*

Volunteers Needed

- *Shoppe Leader: The Village Inn*
- *Leader for each game*
- *Leader for Worship*
- *Leader for "A Quick Ride Through History"*

Camp Meeting

- *Set up the camp meeting indoors or outdoors. Use wooden benches for pews or let people spread quilts on the ground.*
- *Set up an altar area in the front of the space.*

The Village Inn

Supplies: *baskets, wooden bowls, iron skillets, teapots, and churns*

- *Use the Village Inn set up from Session 1.*

✦ Make Apple Cake

Supplies: *ingredients for cake, large bowl, spoon, fork, measuring cups and spoons, muffin tins, cupcake papers*

SAY: When it was time to dry apples, make applesauce, or make apple butter, friends and neighbors in the American colonies often came together for an apple bee. At the apple bee people peeled and cored the apples. Young people would try to peel the apple so that skin came off in one long piece. They would throw the peels over their shoulders onto the floor. Then they'd look to see what letters the peelings looked like. The letters were supposed to be the first letters of the names of the men or women they would marry.

- *Peel and chop apples.*
- *Have the children wash their hands.*
- *Use the recipe below with the children and their parents.*

Apple Cake

1 cup sugar	¼ cup shortening
1 egg	1 cup flour
1 tsp. baking soda	1 tsp. cinnamon
¼ tsp. salt	2 cups chopped raw apple
½ cup raisins	½ cup milk

nuts (use only if no one in your group is allergic to them)

- *Preheat oven at 350 degrees.*
- *Have the children measure the sugar and shortening and place in a large bowl. Stir the sugar and shortening together with a fork.*
- *Beat one egg and stir into mixture.*
- *Have the children measure and add flour, baking soda, cinnamon, and salt to the mixture. Stir well.*
- *Have the children measure and add apples, raisins, and nuts. Mix together.*
- *Line muffin tins with cupcake papers. Pour batter into muffin tins and bake 20 minutes. Makes about 12 cupcakes.*

Always check for allergies before handling or serving food to your children.

The Village Square

- *Provide an open area inside or outside.*
- *Set up several games in the village square for the children and their guests to enjoy.*

SAY: The village square or the market square was an open area where farmers brought their fruits, vegetables, and animals to sell. The square was often used for public celebrations like the king's birthday. The militia practiced on the square. Some people brought cows and sheep to graze. It was also the place where people came together for public games like seeing how fast a team of men could saw a log in half, who could catch a greased pig, or who could climb a greased pole. Children and adults could watch a puppet show or a cockfight.

✦ Fire!

Supplies: *play houses or houses made from large appliance boxes, cardboard for flames, strapping tape or duct tape, buckets, water, towels*

- *Place two houses at one end of the outside play area. Use plastic play houses (the kind made for preschoolers) or large appliance boxes. If you use boxes, cut windows and doors out of the sides of each box. Make large flames out of cardboard. Attach the flames to the back of each house with strapping tape or duct tape.*

SAY: When John was five years old, the rectory caught on fire. Everyone escaped the fire except John. Susanna was standing outside with her other children when she saw John in the second story window of the house. A man climbed on the shoulders of another man and snatched John out of the burning house through the window. John's parents felt that God had saved him for a special purpose. They called John "a brand plucked from the burning."

- *Tell the children that the house is John Wesley's home at Epworth.*
- *Have the children stand in two lines to make bucket brigades. Each line should start at a house. Partially fill two buckets with water. Set a bucket at the end of each line (away from the houses).*
- *Shout, "Fire! Fire! Fire!"*
- *Have the last child in line pick up the bucket and pass it to the child in front of him or her. Let the children continue passing the bucket of water to the front of the line as quickly as they can. Have the child at the front of the line pour the water onto the house.*
- *To make the game a little wetter, have more than one bucket of water to pass down the lines.*

Have towels available.

✦ Jump Ropes

Supplies: *jump ropes*

SAY: Boys played with jumping ropes more often than girls. The boys were supposed to jump with their shoes on so they did not wear holes in their stockings.

- *Provide jump ropes, and let the children play.*

❖ *Soap Bubbles*

Supplies: *soap bubble solution*

SAY: One of the things children in the 1700s did for fun was blow soap bubbles.

- *Let the children enjoy blowing soap bubbles.*

❖ *Marbles*

Supplies: *marbles, optional: masking tape*

SAY: One of the many games played with marbles was called "Taw." The taw was a line drawn in the dirt. A circle was made behind the taw. The players placed all their marbles but one in the circle. They shot the marble from behind the taw into the circle. The goal was to knock the other marbles out of the circle.

- *Go outside and draw the taw and circle in the dirt. Or use masking table to make the taw and circle on the floor.*
- *Provide marbles, and let the game begin.*

Worship

Supplies: *Hymnbooks or Hymns (pp. 34-35), "A Quick Ride Through History" participation pageant (see pages 85-88)*

- *Invite everyone to come gather for the camp meeting.*
- *Begin with singing. Have the children sing and sign "Be Present at Our Table, Lord." Sing favorite Wesley hymns.*
- *Give a short explanation of camp meetings.*

SAY: Camp meetings were times for many people to come together for worship and fellowship. Camp meetings were usually held once or twice a year. Sometimes as many as one thousand people would come to the meetings. Families would set up camp and stay for five to ten days. People would meet together for hours at a time. The best preacher in the area would preach, and people would sing hymns. Hundreds of people would become Christians at the camp meetings.

- *Choose a child to read the Bible verse: "Therefore, go and make disciples of all nations" (Matthew 28:19).*
- *Enjoy "A Quick Ride Through History" participation pageant (p. 85-88).*
- *Present offerings for mission project.*
- *Thank volunteers.*
- *Say a closing prayer.*
- *Enjoy eating the apple cake muffins.*

A Quick Ride Through History

A Participation Pageant

A participation pageant is a short drama that is not rehearsed. The leader reads the script and invites people from the audience to come to the front where they become the characters on the spot. The characters do not have any lines; they form a tableau (frozen picture) of the words the leader is reading. The leader will cue the audience when they are to make a verbal response.

Leader: Let's take a quick ride through history. Put on your tricorn hat *(pantomime putting on hat)* or your best bonnet *(pantomime putting on bonnet)*, throw your saddlebag over your horse, and get ready to ride! Everyone ready? Then say, "Giddy up!"

Audience: Giddy up!

Leader: Our ride begins with a stop at Epworth Rectory, the boyhood home of John Wesley. Who would like to play the part of John Wesley at age five? *(Pick a child.)* Come to the front and take your position. *(Have the child come to the front. Have a sturdy wooden box for the child to stand on.)* When John Wesley was five years old, he and his family lived in Epworth. John's father, Samuel, was the preacher for the town. Who wants to be Samuel Wesley? *(Choose a child or adult.)* Come to the front. *(Have Samuel Wesley kneel near John.)* John's mother was Susanna Wesley. She had nineteen children. Who wants to be Susanna Wesley? *(Choose a child or adult.)* Come to the front. *(Have Susanna stand behind Samuel. Instruct her to look frightened.)* One night the Wesley home caught on fire. Everyone but John escaped the fire. Susanna and Samuel watched as John came to the second story window. The house was covered with flames! Everyone yell, "Fire! Fire! Fire!"

Audience: Fire! Fire! Fire!

Leader: Two neighbors came to the rescue. One neighbor stood on the shoulders of another neighbor and pulled John out of the window. Samuel called his son "a brand plucked from the burning." Let's have a round of applause for John, Samuel, and Susanna. *(Lead audience in clapping, have actors return to their seats.)*

Leader: Now, everyone back on your horses, it's time to ride on.
Everyone say, "Giddy up!"

Audience: Giddy up!

Leader: John grew into quite a scholar. He attended Oxford University and became a clergyman in the Church of England. His brother, Charles, also attended Oxford. While Charles was there, he started a club called the Holy Club. Who would like to be Holy Club members? *(Choose four children.)* Come to the front. *(Have first child stretch and yawn. Have second child pretend to read the Bible. Have third child pretend to pray. Have fourth child pretend to look at watch.)* The Holy Club members followed several rules. They were to get up early, read the Bible, pray, and not waste time. Some people nicknamed the club members "methodists" because the members had a method to everything they did. Everyone shout, "You methodists!"

Audience: You methodists!

Leader: The Holy Club members also worked to help people in need. They visited prisons and spent their own money to buy food and medicines for others. Let's have a round of applause for our Holy Club members. *(Lead audience in clapping, have actors return to their seats.)*

Leader: Now, everyone back on your horses, it's time to ride on.
Everyone say, "Giddy up!"

Audience: Giddy up!

Leader: John and Charles Wesley met a man named General Olgethorpe. He asked the two young men to go with him to a place across the sea called Georgia to tell the people there about Jesus. John and Charles decided to go. Who wants to be John? *(Choose a child.)* Who wants to be Charles? *(Choose a child.)* Come to the front. *(Have the children pretend to row a boat.)* The voyage took four months. John's time in Georgia did not go well. He made many people angry. John decided to go back to England. Everyone shout, "Go home, John!"

Audience: Go home, John!

Leader: Let's have a round of applause for John and Charles. *(Lead audience in clapping, have actors return to their seats.)*

Leader: Now, everyone back on your horses, it's time to ride on.
Everyone say, "Giddy up!"

Audience: Giddy up!

Leader: When John returned to England, he began to doubt his faith. One night, he went to a Moravian meeting on Aldersgate Street. Who wants to be John? (*Choose a child.*) Come to the front. (*Have child stand with hands over his or her heart.*) At that meeting John said, "I felt my heart strangely warmed." He felt God's love. Turn to your neighbor and say, "God loves you!"

Audience: God loves you!

Leader: Let's have a round of applause for John. (*Lead audience in clapping, have actor return to his or her seat.*)

Leader: Now, everyone back on your horses, it's time to ride on. Everyone say, "Giddy up!"

Audience: Giddy up!

Leader: John changed his way of preaching after his Aldersgate experience. Many churches did not want John to preach inside the church buildings. But that did not stop him. John preached on the streets. He preached in the fields. He preached near factories and coal mines. He even preached standing on top of his father's tombstone! Now who wants to be John? (*Choose a child.*) Come to the front. (*Have child stand in place and pretend to ride a horse.*) John started riding his horse from place to place. He preached two or three times every day, seven days a week. He traveled all over England, telling others the good news about Jesus. John Wesley felt that the world was his parish. Everyone say the Bible verse, "Therefore, go and make disciples of all nations" (Matthew 28:19).

Audience: "Therefore, go and make disciples of all nations" (Matthew 28:19).

Leader: Let's have a round of applause for John. (*Lead audience in clapping, have actor return to his or her seat.*)

Leader: Now, everyone back on your horses, it's time to ride on. Everyone say, "Giddy up!"

Audience: Giddy up!

Leader: The Methodist movement crossed the sea to the American colonies. Circuit riders traveled on horseback from town to town, telling others the good news about Jesus. Thomas Coke was sent to America after the War of Independence. Thomas Coke ordained another man, Francis Asbury, to be bishop. Who wants to be Francis Asbury? (*Choose a child.*) Come to the front. (*Have the child pretend to ride a horse.*)

Francis Asbury traveled 275,000 miles, mostly on horseback to tell others the good news about Jesus. Let's help Francis' horse make it to the next town. Everyone pat their legs to make the sound of horses hooves hitting the ground.

Audience: (pat legs)

Leader: Let's have a round of applause for Francis. *(Lead audience in clapping, have actor return to his or her seat.)*

Leader: Now, everyone back on your horses, it's time to ride on.
Everyone say, "Giddy up!"

Audience: Giddy up!

Leader: Other men and women helped the Methodist church to grow in America. Men like Richard Allen, a slave who bought his freedom. He became the first bishop in the African Methodist Episcopal Church. Who wants to be Richard Allen? *(Choose a child to come to the front.)* He welcomed all people into the church. *(Shake hands with child.)*

Leader: And there were men like Jonathan Pointer and John Stewart. Who wants to be Jonathan Pointer? *(Choose a child to come to the front.)* Who wants to be John Stewart? *(Choose a child to come to the front.)* At first the two men didn't get along. But then they spread God's Word to Native Americans. *(Have the two children shake hands with each other.)*

Leader: Now, I think the horses are tired. It's time to stop our quick ride through history. Everyone say, "Whoa, horsey!"

Audience: Whoa, horsey!

Leader: Many others throughout history have spread the good news about Jesus all across world. As United Methodists we believe that the world is our parish. Let's say Matthew 28:19 once again; "Therefore, go and make disciples of all nations."

Audience: "Therefore, go and make disciples of all nations" (Matthew 28:19).

CPSIA information can be obtained
at www.ICGtesting.com
Printed in the USA
LVOW03s1945200416

484582LV00004B/4/P

9 781501 805066